A Cookbook for Katie

Upon the Occasion of Her Marriage
Recipes and Reveries for the Bride

By
Daphne
Simpkins

ISBN: 0615925669
INSB 13: 9780615925660
Library of Congress Control Number: 2013920907
Quotidian Books,
Montgomery, AL

For the Bride

Table of Contents

Introduction: What's for Supper? xi

A Taste of Home: *The Sundays of Summer*..................................xvi

Section 1 The Perfect Food and What's In Your Pantry 1

Cornbread—what you call the perfect food, and I agree 2

Pantry staples you will need to keep on hand 5

Pepper Steak– because this is one of your favorite dishes...............7

Vegetable Beef Soup, which I make in the wintertime 8

Pot Roast or roast with vegetables, which I make year-round.........9

Lola's Peach cobbler, which I think about more than I make 10

French toast, a bad-weather recipe..11

A Taste of Home: *Me.....You*..13

Section 2 The Peanut, the Sweet Potato, Mr. Carver and Your Grandmother...15

Behold The Peanut...16

Aunt Julie's Peanut Butter Cookies—a child's thumbprint seals it in love 18

Aunt Julie's Peanut Butter Cake—her family's favorite birthday cake...19

Lola's Sweet Potato Pie—a recipe she took to the grave but I got it back...22

Aunt Daphne's Praline-Topped Sweet Potatoes—for when you don't have marshmallows..25

Baked Chicken—a mainstay of Sunday dinners...........................26

Baked Turkey—supposedly the Thanksgiving centerpiece..........27

Cornbread Dressing—supposedly the side dish but it steals the limelight..........28

Homemade Cranberry Sauce—inherited from Miss Esther..........31

Coca-Cola Jell-O—your grandmother's signature side dish at Christmas..........32

A Taste of Home: *Two Shakes of a Lamb's Tail*..........33

Section 3 The Egg and I and You..........39

Meringue—you need to know how to top off desserts and nothing is better than meringue..........42

Lemon Meringue Pie—a wedding pie..........44

Cousin Kevin's Divinity—a wedding candy..........46

Egg Salad Sandwiches—for when you have too many eggs on hand and no lunch meat..........48

Egg and Sausage Casserole—when you have overnight guests..........49

A Taste of Home: *A Dog Story*..........52

Section 4 The Onion, the Potato, and Being an Outlaw Cook.....55

Potato Soup –for when you are feeling poorly (or poor)..........58

Suppertime Potato Salad—a main dish that is often wrongly served only as a side dish..........60

Homemade French Fries –the food of love..........61

Aunt Daphne's Corned Beef Hash—no one admits to liking this dish but people eat it..........63

Cousin Kevin's Bacon-Fried Cabbage—for bacon-lovers..........65

The Sounds of Home: *The Secret Language of Married Women*..........67

Section 5 Flour, Gravy and Gallbladders 71

Lola's Southern Woman Gravy—the way Southern women used to make this gravy..73

Aunt Mary Ellen's Gravy—a gravy in process perfected by your Aunt Mary 75

Aunt Guin's Cream Gravy (sometimes called Bird Gravy but not by Texans)..76

Country Fried Steak—a misunderstood entrée.............................76

A Taste Of Home: *That Missing Piece of Nora's Cake*.....................81

Apricot Nectar Cake—the cake to take to a house of mourning... 86

Section 6 Comfort Foods 89

Delicious Scrambled eggs—the really good kind 92

Chicken Noodle Soup—because you love this soup! 93

Chicken Pot Pie—oft forgotten and it shouldn't be......................94

Chicken Salad—inexpensive to make and costly to buy already made 96

Bride's Delight—"It's not entirely horrible" you said. 97

Homemade Cocoa—for when you are alone and need company... 98

The Sounds of Home: *Fever Pitch*...100

Section 7 What to take to a Potluck or Fellowship Supper......... 103

Chicken Poppy Seed Casserole—a dish that won't be served in heaven 104

Aunt Daphne's Fried Chicken—a dish that will be served in heaven 108

Aunt Judy's I-Love-You-Arms-Wide-Open Lasagna—represents the love of heaven 111

Cherry Cobbler—a troubling dessert that can make other women see red 112
Strawberry Pie—so you will know what a pie like this is supposed to taste like 113
Baked Ham—for breakfast Christmas morning 114
A Taste of Home: *Church Lady Chicken Supreme* 117

Section 8 The Katie Days and Snacks 121
The Bride-To-Be as a Baby 124
The Bride-To-Be in Her Bath 127
The Bride-To-Be At Home with Her Aunt 130
The Bride-To-Be Dreams of Heaven 134
The Bride-To-Be Goes Shopping 137
The Bride-To-Be and Figuring Time 140
The Bride-To-Be Becomes Herself 142
The Bride-To-Be Goes To College 145

Section 9 Every day is a good day—recipes from Miss Esther 153
Esther's Handed-Down Chicken and Dumplings 154
Esther's Pimiento Cheese Sandwich Spread 154
Esther's Applesauce Cake 155
Esther's Basic Apple Pie 156
Esther's Chocolate Sheath Cake 157
Esther's French Fudge 158
Esther's Gingerbread 159
Esther's Pecan Cake 160
A Taste of Home: *Riding with the windows down, living with the windows open* 162

Section 10 Your Signature Dish **165**

Mildred Budge's Signature Jelly Cake– invented by me 168

Pineapple Filling– because sometimes you need a filling like this 170

Mildred Budge's Favorite Almond-Flavored Pound Cake—in memory of your grandmother 170

Mildred Budge's Butter Pecan Cake, would make a great wedding cake without the pecans 171

Aunt Daphne's Christmas Fudge—not as hard to make as people think 174

Your Mama's Signature Pecan Pie, and served by a belle of the South, your mama 176

Aunt Julie's Coffee Cake– but it's really more about the coffee 178

Cousin Kevin's Simple White Sauce– simplicity matters and he proves it here 178

Guin's Date Loaf Candy—much better than my fudge, though no one believes me 179

Cousin Lola's Chocolate Chip Muffins—made by the best cook in the family, really 180

At Home Everywhere I Go: *The Bride's Room* 183

About the gatherer of recipes, Aunt Daphne **191**

Introduction

What's for Supper?

Do you remember your grandmother?

I can still hear my mother talking about cooking though she's been in heaven a very long time now.

When your grandmother made a meal others really enjoyed, they would say something like, "That was wonderful, Lola!" and she would reply, "I know. It was really good."

Lola Morris, your grandmother, was a good cook and she knew it, but your grandmother wasn't a great cook.

None of us in the family is, really, except your cousin Lola Leigh.

We will never be on TV teaching others how to cook, except, maybe, Lola Leigh.

Our recipes are rarely original except when we leave out an ingredient because we don't have that on hand and don't want to go to the grocery store to get it.

We learn about cooking and making certain dishes from our mistakes and from other people mostly, and we do not have sophisticated palates. We like lots of sugar and lots of salt and strong, very hot coffee. We eat until we get full, moan something about our eyes being bigger than our stomachs, and then we eat some more. We like to eat. Those who don't really enjoy food tend to be the ones who like to drink. Most of our family mainly like to eat, and we keep the food cooking and on the table. That is the ultimate test of what a cook does. *Is it good enough to eat? Do people eat it?*

If people are consistently eating your cooking, you are a successful cook.

You may become a better cook than all of us—it wouldn't be hard to do that, actually. We're quite ordinary in our skills and menus. But if you don't exceed the rest of us and your Southern heritage of boiling vegetables for too long and frying most anything, I hope that you will share the laudable virtue that your grandmother, your mother, and the rest of the dependable cooks in the family lived out as a daily responsibility: we do the cooking when we feel like it and we do the cooking when we don't feel like it and we stack the dishwasher and we unstack the dishwasher and we make the coffeepot for the next morning the night before so that it's ready when our feet hit the floor to start the next day of cooking.

That's ultimately the goal that a homemaker lives up to (not the business about making the coffeepot—the cooking); and after years of doing this, you will most likely hear others say, "She is a good cook."

That expression does not refer to a single signature dish or any superior level of culinary excellence; it's about cooking and cooking and cooking and answering the question "What's for supper?" over and over again with a meal of some kind that your family will eat.

Don't be sidetracked by the discussion of whether cooking is also a man's job. Your husband will provide enough of the meals—society has evolved that way– and you can solve that problem between the two of you (it is really nobody else's business). But when love takes hold—really takes hold—you don't have so many problems about dividing up the work.

Don't let the way the world talks about the division of duties between the sexes make you see the work of building a home the way it doesn't need to be seen.

Love means you are trying to make a life and when a job needs to be done like the cooking, just do it. Don't calculate whose turn or whose job it is. If you ever get to a point where you think that love has caused you to take on more work than you think is your fair share, solve the problem but don't blame the other person because making a home is simply a great deal of work. Hold the demands of life itself accountable for being hard work. Hold yourself accountable for loving to the point of self-sacrifice, and then don't beat yourself or anyone else up later if you get tired of loving extravagantly, because that's another way to see self-sacrifice. You will cook and clean up. You will take out the garbage. You will change the sheets. You will bite your tongue upon occasion because after a while, when starry-eyed romance has faded to the cold view of realism, you might discover that he has patterns of speech and other habits that strike you as annoying. As soon as you begin to see anything about him that you think needs to be corrected, you would be wise to wonder which of your habits is now driving him crazy. If you ever start thinking, 'how irritating, how immature, how thoughtless'—remember this: Everyone is immature, and everyone is irritating. We just all have different ways of being immature and irritating. If you want him to forgive you for your unreasonable, thoughtless, selfish, immature, and irritating behaviors, let go of judging his. It's easy to do if you just decide to do that. A lot of getting along with other people is more about making a decision that you want to get along and then doing whatever is necessary to keep the peace.

I was reading in the book of James this morning from THE MESSAGE that wisdom isn't proven by showing how smart you are but how able you are to get along with other people. Isn't that a refreshing way to think about wisdom? Wisdom is knowing how to get along with other people, and it's never more important than inside a marriage that, at first, is defined by passion and a series of big changes and, later, gets defined mostly wrongly by routine and a desire not to change. You will have to be willing to change inside the routine of building a life that often revolves around eating and cooking. Learn to love the work of that because the life that gets built deserves the effort—and respect.

Decide to love without complaining. Be willing to spend yourself extravagantly. The rewards are enormous even if the meals are routine and the ingredients ordinary. We talk about our company meals and parties, but it is mostly the day-to-day dining that creates our feelings about cooking.

So back to the question, "What's for supper?"

Often you will be the one who answers that question about what's for supper by looking into your pantry or refrigerator about an hour before suppertime to see what you can pull together. Or maybe your husband will. But I'm not writing this cookbook for him. I am writing it for you, Beloved, because you asked me to assemble some family recipes to take with you in your travels as you make your first home as a military wife. You can see into the future, and you will want a taste of home. So will he.

Your husband and a wide-ranging number of other people—some you haven't met yet– will join you at your growing family's table that is often the nexus of home life.

That table is a special place. History gets made and told there while the suppers are being eaten.

I have your grandmother's oak table in my kitchen. I grew up eating at that oak table sitting on hardwood benches that I do not use anymore since I inherited the table from your grandmother too many years ago. Those hardwood benches hurt! I have chairs now, but the table is the same. I dust it sometimes the way your grandmother did in about the same frequency. (We don't like to dust in our family, and we just don't do it unless company is coming.)

Your grandmother would approve and understand why I got rid of those unforgiving benches because she was practical the way that I am practical, and she liked comfort more than elegance. Mama kept the benches because her husband had bought them and had taken pride in them. Your granddaddy sat at the head of that table in a chair, and he didn't really know how hard the benches were. We didn't complain, and your grandmother did not get rid of the benches because doing that would have hurt her husband's feelings. There's a lot I could tell you about your grandmother. But here's a story about her and your grandfather that was published back when we sat on the hardwood benches together.

I am giving you this story, Beloved, because eating and recipes always come with stories. That's one of the reasons they taste good.

A Taste of Home....

THE SUNDAYS OF SUMMER

"We don't know what's got into her, Tommy. She's been shoveling dirt to fill in the potholes in the road and picking up sticks in the woods."

"Baby," My uncle Tommy said, turning to me. "That's something men are supposed to do."

"Yes, sir," I agreed. "And, if I could find one to do it better than I do and as cheaply, I'd turn the work over to him."

They all nodded approvingly. I had not lost my mind yet. I smiled my good niece, sensible daughter smile and began to unload my cart load of sticks while they said their good-byes. My uncle Tommy had driven out for an afternoon of Sunday visiting, and now he was leaving.

After he drove off, Mother said, "We've still got some coffee inside."

"Wouldn't mind a cup," I admitted.

"Don't you snap off your fingernails doing that kind of work?" My mother asked suddenly.

"Yes, ma'am. Broke them all off down to the quick. Can't have long fingernails and do any real work."

"How much longer do you figure on working the woods and fixing the road?" Dad inquired.

"Let's see," I calculated aloud. "I've lost nineteen pounds and I want to shed another eleven. At five pounds a month, I figure two more months."

"That's all right then, as long as you've got a good reason to be out in this heat," my father approved.

We go inside their house together where the aroma of freshly brewed coffee commingles with the fragrance of my Uncle Tommy's new cologne that he is wearing since he began dating his high school sweetheart again. A widower for too long, he is in love again and we are all happy for him. That fast, though I have just seen him, I miss him. I wish I had let the sticks and potholes in our long dirt driveway go and gone inside while Uncle Tommy was here and sipping coffee at the table and talking about what was going on with him. My mother will tell me in time—maybe not today—but soon. "Your Uncle Tommy has fallen in love....."

But not yet.

My mother pours the coffee. Her teaspoon hovers nostalgically near the sugar bowl. She knows I am dieting, but she thinks it's a sin to drink coffee black on some days—like when we're all together. We're together every day. Every day is potentially a celebration for her—a reason to add a spoonful of sugar to rejoice. "How about a good old heaping spoonful of sugar?" she asks wistfully.

To say no would change her view of home life, of me, of the world.

"Thanks. I could use the energy," I say.

Happily, she adds the sugar (I am forgiven the abuse of my fingernails), stirs vigorously, and brings my cup to me.

"You've done some fine work out there," Dad commends.

"It feels good to work hard," I confess. "Makes my muscles feel reliable. What have you been doing?" I ask, and I slurp. (We are a family of slurpers.)

"You know us. We stay pretty busy. Been talking with Tommy all afternoon. Have you seen your sister today?"

"Not since yesterday. Probably see Mary Ellen in a few minutes when she comes out to check on her fruit trees."

"I think she just planted those trees so that she would have an excuse to be outside," my mother remarks innocently. My mother knows very well that my picking up sticks and filling in potholes in our long dirt drive that we traverse together is not a weight loss plan, really, but, like my sister's examination of her fruit trees, a reason to be outside on a summer day.

I do not mind that Mother sees through me. She often understands me. I slurp her sweetened coffee in gratitude.

"You gonna work some more today?" Dad asks.

"Not this evening. Gonna head home and finish the new Spenser novel. Did you know that people eat cornbread muffins for breakfast in Boston?"

"Northerners are different, but I can see cornbread muffins making a good breakfast."

"Spenser can cook—a man!" I waited a beat, and added, "Of course, he is a fictional character."

My father smiles at my teasing because he does not cook and waits for me to hug him hard as an apology for leaving him. He never wants me to go. I never want to leave him. We embrace fiercely. "You're always in a hurry," he chides me.

"I learned all of my bad habits from you," I reply, kissing the top of his balding head.

I carry my cup to the sink, and pivot slowly, taking pleasure in the late afternoon sunlight as it falls in through the panel of kitchen windows. My parents glow in it. The light falls upon their lovely, homegrown faces. Their hands rest together on the oak tabletop. Like the hospitality of a summer day, my parents' shadows cast upon the wall appear larger than life—welcoming and long lasting, keeping time in a way that a clock cannot.

"Thanks for the coffee. When you cook some pinto beans, will you let me know?"

"Might have to call on you on the telephone."

"If I hear it ringing, I will answer it," I promise.

I head down the dirt road toward my house and my sister's which is on the other side. Mary Ellen is sitting in her swing and she calls to me, "Do you want a cup of coffee?"

"Why not?" I reply, abandoning my empty cart.

When Mary Ellen returns, we sit and slurp together. She taps the ground with her foot, establishing a gentle rhythm in the swing.

"Time sure goes by fast, doesn't it?"

"Sure does," I agree. "We better stop and enjoy it before we wake up dead."

Mary Ellen murmurs something inaudible. I don't need to hear it exactly to know what she has said. The sky gets pink, then grey. We swing together in silence as the summer day ends.

Beloved,

Here come the recipes and some other cooking tips. The recipes are not fancy, but they're good. Many generations of your family passed along these basic recipes for everyday meals. I tried to explain how to make them so they would taste like home. There may be some mistakes in the recipes, Beloved. That's the way life is. Approach these recipes the way you do other people's advice about how to live the married life (including mine)—with a grain of salt.

Section 1

The Perfect Food and What's In Your Pantry

What's in this section:

Cornbread

Staples you will need in your pantry

Pepper Steak

Homemade Vegetable Beef Soup

Pot Roast or roast with vegetables

Peach cobbler

French toast

A Taste of Home: *Me.....You*

CORNBREAD

What you will need:

A seasoned iron skillet, which I have already given you

Some cooking oil (I use Crisco.)

Buttermilk corn meal mix (Martha White)

An egg

Some milk

The right bowl

A sturdy spoon

Beloved,

It surprised me that you did not like the crust on cornbread since I go to a good amount of trouble to create the perfect crust for my cornbread, and I am terribly vain about my cornbread crusts. You have been eating the inside of my cornbread for as long as you first announced years ago that "Cornbread is the perfect food," and you have not yet developed an appetite for the crusty part. Maybe one day you will—or your husband will. People can have very strong feelings and preferences about cornbread.

Should that day come when you understand that the outside of the cornbread is as good as the inside, here's how you make a perfect crust on the perfect food.

Pour some oil in the iron skillet that I gave you.

I have never known a woman in our family to measure the amount of oil needed. Cooking oil thins out when it heats up, so it becomes more liquid than you think when you first cover the bottom of the iron skillet.

To do this comfortably, hold the handle of the skillet and rotate the pan so that the oil coats the sides, too. A hot skillet coated in oil creates the crust and causes the cornbread to fall out easily when it's done. Over time, this process helps to keep your skillet seasoned.

You may have to make a couple of practice pans of cornbread to determine how much oil you prefer in your batter. More oil is better than not enough, but too much oil creates strange little holes across the top. The little potholes don't hurt anything, but they don't look good.

Turn your oven on to 425 degrees unless you are timing the cornbread to come out when the supper is ready. In that case you can reduce the heat some, but at that high heat of 425 degrees cornbread gets done in about ten minutes if your pan is the size for two eaters.

My point is for you to let the oil heat up in the pan while the oven preheats. When the oven is finished pre-heating, you use two cloths to take the pan out of the oven and carry it over to pour the hot grease into your cornbread mixture. Watch out. It will sizzle and splatter. Use a long-handled spoon to avoid hot grease burning you while you stir the oil thoroughly into the batter. That heated oil is part of your liquid required for your recipe, and cornbread can be baked from a thick batter or a thin batter. I prefer a thin batter because I like a lighter cornbread. The more liquid, the thinner the batter. I have seen other cooks who made their batter and let it sit on the counter for a few minutes while waiting on the oven to heat need to add some water just to thin it out. You can do that—or add a bit more milk. Cornbread batter is forgiving.

After the oil is mixed in, immediately pour your batter into that hot skillet. It should sizzle some more and begin to bubble around the sides. It is lovely to behold. When that happens, you know your crust is going to be perfect.

How do you make the batter?

Figure out which mix you like. I use Martha White. I do not measure anything. I have a cornbread bowl. It's that white chipped bowl that holds about three and a half cups of anything. I pour about a cup and a half of mix into the bowl. Stir in the egg. I pour milk until the batter is thick and thoroughly moistened. I leave it like that until the oil is hot in the pre-heated oven. When I pour on the oil that usually makes the batter soupy. That's good. Pour the batter into your hot skillet.

Transfer the skillet back to the hot oven pronto.

Place your mixing bowl in the sink and run some water in it because that cornmeal dries hard; and if you wait to rinse it, that bowl will be hard to scrub. (The same is true of cups from which you have sipped milk or the skillet you use to scramble eggs. Rinse those quickly or pay the consequences in scrubbing later.)

The cornbread is done when you can reach in and tap the center with your finger, and it doesn't cave in. Baked cornbread doesn't spring back the way a perfectly baked cake will. Cornbread taps hard to the touch when it's done.

Turn off the oven.

Use two cloths to bring out the skillet again because the handle is scary hot.

Let the cornbread cool a minute or so while you set the table.

Then, run a butter knife around the edge of the cornbread to loosen it from the skillet, tip the skillet over a serving plate, and let the cornbread fall onto it. It will smell good. Serve with softened butter.

By the way, on a hot day when you do not want to turn on the oven and heat up your kitchen, you can fry cornbread batter and make small cornbread pancakes. You make that same batter about the same way but don't add the oil. Just put about a quarter inch of oil in a frying skillet (not the iron skillet this time). Get the frying skillet hot and then drop tablespoons of cornbread batter into the hot oil. When the edges begin to brown and the centers have bubbled (about a minute or so—not long!), flip the little cornbread pancakes. This version of cornbread takes about three-four minutes, and these corncakes are served like silver-dollar pancakes. Add some butter or not. The more oil you use in the skillet the less likely you will need any butter at all. Some people call these hoecakes.

Cornbread goes with:

Beans—just about any kind, and if you have chow-chow you can call that supper and be happy. (The restaurant Cracker Barrel sells a very nice chow-chow.)

Soup—just about any kind

Left-overs when you want to freshen up the dinner from the night before with something hot and good

The Pantry....

Here's what you need for a pantry that can see you through a bad-weather event or a case of the flu:

Cornflakes

Rice Krispies

Oatmeal

Marshmallows (for the Rice Krispie treats that I consider a staple)

Saltine Crackers

A bag of dried beans (pinto, Great Northern)

Pasta—all sorts

Jars of marinara or other red sauces

Dried Parmesan

Chili and assorted soups

Canned chicken

Canned corned beef

Honey

Sugar

Evaporated milk

Cocoa

Cooking oil

Flour—plain and self-rising

Jelly

Nutmeg

Cinnamon

Salt

Pepper

Baking Soda

Peanut Butter

Apple Cider Vinegar

Syrup (Alaga)

Bisquick

A large can of pineapple and/or peaches

Pepper Steak

Here's a list of the ingredients:

Beef strips

Beef broth

Onions

Mushrooms

Bell peppers

Tomatoes

Rice

Directions:

This economical recipe suits just about everyone. Choose your beef strips. Sometimes beef packaged in slices like this is labeled beef fajita strips. Brown them in a skillet. After the beef is browned, add some water and maybe some beef broth (or something like that—there are many brown sauces available now). Then, add chopped onions, sliced mushrooms (a lot of these), a handful of cherry tomatoes or quartered full-size tomatoes, and when you are about twenty minutes from serving the dish, toss on lots of sliced, multi-colored bell peppers. I use orange, yellow, red and green. It is beautiful!

Serve with rice. It usually makes enough for left-overs. Pepper Steak is even better the next night. I sometimes reserve a bell pepper or two to add to the left-overs so that the peppers are freshened, and I love bell peppers so there are never enough for me.

You can mix and match the veggies to suit yourself, but you really need the onions.

Vegetable Beef Soup

What you need:

2-3 lbs. or so of beef cubes or chunks—lean

Potatoes

Onions

Carrots

Beef broth

Bay leaves

A couple of cans of diced tomatoes

A can of corn

Salt and pepper

Directions:

This all-purpose soup is good on a cold day, and it freezes pretty well. You can make it on the stove or in your crock pot.

If you are making it on the stove, brown the beef. Add the can (or two) of tomatoes. Add some beef broth. Add the bay leaves. I use about five.

Remember to remove the bay leaves before you serve the soup. I have heard that if you swallow a bay leaf it will kill you. I don't believe that, but I still worry about it. Add water. Add onions, potatoes, and carrots. Salt and pepper as you go. Add the corn near the end of cooking so the kernels won't get too soft.

Serve with crackers or cornbread.

Pot Roast (with vegetables)

What you need:

The right cooking pot, which you will have to figure out for yourself. But look for a heavy-bottomed pan with a lid that closes securely to keep the steam inside.

The cut of roast you prefer (sirloin tip is usually foolproof)

Potatoes (five or six)

Carrots (as many as you like)

Onions (probably two)

Directions:

The easiest dish in the world to make is a pot roast. Buy your preferred cut of meat. I like a sirloin tip though I cook eye of round now, too, but it needs some fat on one side of it to keep it moist while cooking.

On top of the stove, get your pan sizzling hot, and sear each side of the roast. Salt and pepper afterwards. Place the bottom side down; add a bit of water—about an inch in the pan—cover and simmer on low until it reaches the level of doneness. I like my roast well cooked. Some people like it pink.

Cook your vegetables on the side if you cook the roast this way. Let the natural juices be the accompaniment or make the Southern Woman Gravy described in chapter 5.

If you want to make this more simply, just place your roast bottom side down in a big roasting dish. Toss in chopped onions, carrots, big chunks of potatoes, salt and pepper. Add some water to create steam, and cover with a big piece of tin foil and crimp it very tightly around the edges to keep the steam in. Place it in the oven on 325 degrees, and let it bake for a couple of hours while you are in church. You will come home to a proper Sunday lunch.

Serve with sweet iced tea.

Lola's Easy Peach Cobbler

Here's what you need:

One cup of self-rising flour

One large can of sliced peaches

One stick of melted butter or margarine

One cup of whole milk

One cup of sugar

Directions:

Take a Pyrex dish—9 by 13—and pour in your milk, the sugar, the flour, and the melted butter. Stir that together. Add the can of peaches with the syrup. Bake until the cobbler is bubbly and the crust forms on the top.

Serve hot with vanilla ice cream or just serve it hot.

Your granddaddy loved this peach cobbler. Most men do. And you can use the same recipe and change out the fruit. As long as the fruit has any kind of syrup it will make a cobbler. As you can see, other than the can of peaches, flour, and sugar from the pantry, your refrigerator should have the eggs, the milk, the butter or margarine. It is a handy, hot dessert that tastes like home.

By now you can see that having a pantry stocked in basic goods means you can put a supper together pretty speedily.

French Toast

What you will need:

Bread (slightly stale or a half loaf that you froze because you brought a fresh loaf in and you didn't want to throw away good bread)

Eggs

Milk

Butter

Syrup

Vanilla extract

Nutmeg

Confectioner's sugar, if you have a sweet tooth or like it pretty

A bit of fruit—any kind, really

Kevin says, "I sometimes add some orange zest to mine."

Directions:

Beat two-three eggs in a bowl for about four-five pieces of toast

Add a splash of milk

Add a teaspoon of Vanilla extract

Add nutmeg–as much as you like and more than you think you need

Once you have your egg mixture, stack your slices of bread beside that bowl because it is about to get messy.

Melt sufficient butter in your skillet to cover it with a little extra to soak into the bread. Get it pretty hot.

As soon as the skillet is hot but your butter is not scorching, dip each slice of bread in the egg mixture. Move quickly. Coat both sides of the bread with the egg mixture. Transfer the egg-coated bread quickly to the hot skillet so that your butter doesn't have a chance to darken, and fry the bread in the butter on both sides. Make sure you cook all of the egg!

Place the French toast on a plate and sprinkle with confectioner's sugar and some fruit. Drizzle on your favorite syrup. I like Alaga syrup because I think it tastes better than any other brand.

You can also use peanut butter on French toast, if you like. I am not a fan, but some people like it.

Peanut butter—speaking of peanut butter your Aunt Julie makes Mrs. Helms' Peanut Butter cake, and it is what your Uncle Jody usually wants for his birthday. You will find that recipe in the next chapter.

A Taste of Home....

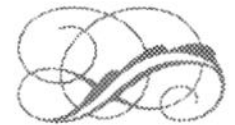

Me....You

After my company left, I started the laundry, surprised at the quantity of it. For when company comes to visit, forgotten bath towels and dish towels buried deep in drawers are pulled out and used. You need them all when you have a lot of company. I washed load after load of laundry, folding as I went, stopping when I discovered an old-timey dish towel that had infiltrated my linen supply from houses I have helped clean out after the death of the person who had lived there.

The one I held in my hand was bigger than more modern cloths we call store-bought. I don't know when I have heard the distinction made that something is store-bought because most things are. This cloth had not come from a store. It was from a former bride's hope chest.

This dish cloth was homemade, oversized, a soft white well-washed cotton fabric, and it was hand embroidered in the corner with words and images: a blue spoon, a red fork, and two words had been carefully embroidered in purple: Me....You.

The simplicity of those two words rather than the usual assortment of wordy clichés surprised me, existing in their very simplicity as the barest form of very good poetry. They named the truth of a home, a relationship, a love story that to my idea of romantic sentiment has never been told a better way.

I held the cloth in my hands and folded it tenderly, smoothing the words, remembering when love stories had sounded like that, looked as simple as that, and were so often associated with home and hearth—Me... You—rather than the glamorized and frequently disappointing words of passion and desire that can burn brightly and then fade away and leave behind, confusion, heartache, and disillusionment.

Now I'm old enough to know that heartache occurs in most love stories; no one loves well without experiencing heartache, but that isn't the same as heartbreak or broken trust or simply throwing in the towel because the work of loving someone else got too hard for the two of you.

That ambition to love well doesn't become impossible because of the You that we have chosen to love but because we focus too much on the Me in the relationship.

The towel was both homey and romantic. Like a pressed flower from a memorable dance. Like a snippet of a love poem discovered tucked in a Bible. Like a love story I witnessed at the eye doctor's recently.

While waiting for an appointment to get my eyes checked, I witnessed an old man also waiting see his aged wife emerge from the exam room. He rose to his feet instantly and called out jubilantly, "Yonder she comes!"

As if his seasoned bride was a queen. As if we should all rise and applaud because the woman he loved had entered the room. As if he really, really loved her.

I knew who he was after that, and I knew who they were as a couple. He wasn't just waiting on her. He was waiting for her—always had, always would.

I could have wrapped this oversized towel around them and covered those two old lovers in the simple truth of what "Me....You" means. Doing so would have proclaimed the truth lived out and promised in the words of love and commitment they vowed years ago: "I do."

Section 2

The Peanut, the Sweet Potato, Mr. Carver and Your Grandmother

What's in this section:

A recipe for a good life from George Washington Carver

Aunt Julie's Peanut Butter Cookies

Aunt Julie's Peanut Butter Cake

Lola's Sweet Potato Pie

Aunt Daphne's Praline-Topped Sweet Potatoes

Baked Chicken

Baked Turkey

Aunt Daphne's Cornbread Dressing

Homemade Cranberry Sauce

Coca-Cola Jell-O

A Taste of Home: *Two Shakes of a Lamb's Tail*

BEHOLD THE PEANUT.

Did you study the peanut in school?

We did.

It is a lowly edible legume that I most often eat as peanut butter.

Sometimes, when I am trying to curtail my appetite, I scoop out a big tablespoonful of peanut butter and eat it like an ice cream cone. I love peanut butter, but I never think about peanut butter without remembering one of my great heroes, George Washington Carver. He was an educator over at Tuskegee Institute and a great spirit here and now in heaven.

There are schools named after Mr. Carver, and there should be.

Mr. Carver helped to rebuild the agricultural industry especially among the poor farming regions around us by writing educational bulletins and going out to visit people to tell them about crop rotation and how switching out crops can replenish the soil. (Remember, Beloved, that one must do that in daily life as well. When you find yourself feeling sluggish, tired, or trapped, don't blame someone else. Change your routine.)

But the story I most enjoy about Mr. Carver is how he, a scientist, stopped before entering into his laboratory to ask God to help him see or discover what he needed to understand about the peanut and the sweet potato and the soybean because in developing the uses for these agricultural products he accomplished two big goals: he helped farmers find new markets for what they had to sell and he validated in a scientific environment the highly unlikely process of relying upon God for help to see what he needed to see. In short, Mr. Carver, a scientist, proved that revelations from God happen.

At least they happened to him.

He had about 300 revelations about the peanut.

He had over 200 revelations about the sweet potato.

He had over a hundred uses/revelations about the soybean before it would become the bean of the century.

Additionally, my darling, Mr. Carver taught students the Bible in the evenings. In the teaching of the Bible, Mr. Carver developed his own moral code—a recipe for living well inside the faith that allows an artist–for he was a painter as well as a scientist– to validate God's goodness with answers to unlikely prayers.

Mr. Carver's recipe for a Good Life:

Be clean both inside and out.

Neither look up to the rich nor down on the poor.

Lose, if need be, without squealing.

Win without bragging.

Always be considerate of women, children and older people.

Be too brave to lie.

Be too generous to cheat.

Take your share of the world and let others take theirs.

I love this last idea because it addresses the problems of gluttony and covetousness—two old fashioned words that are current epidemics. Beware of eating what's on your plate with your eye on a second helping; and when you find yourself dissatisfied with life in general, be aware that you most likely want more than your share. There is such a thing as one's fair portion in life. Learn to be content with it and grateful for it, and you will be a happier human being than most.

We all fall prey to wanting more than our fair share of anything in our lifetimes. Learn to manage both conditions in yourself, and you will be able to enjoy your share of what's for supper and be glad for others to have theirs.

Weave this idea into your life by attaching it to simple activities. When you make a peanut butter sandwich, remember Mr. Carver and his principles and be too brave to lie to yourself about what you know about your own appetites and how they do or don't fit inside a world of fair shares.

Consider the peanut and let it remind you of lowly portions. Take your share of the peanuts and let others take theirs.

Aunt Julie's Peanut Butter Cookies

Ingredients:

½ cup butter or margarine

1 cup granulated sugar

½ cup brown sugar

½ cup peanut butter (creamy)

1 egg

¾ teaspoon baking soda

½ teaspoon baking powder

1 ¼ cups all-purpose flour

¼ teaspoon salt

Directions:

Cream butter, sugars and peanut butter. Add the other ingredients and the egg. Shape into small balls of dough. Most people use a fork to make a crisscross pattern across the top. Aunt Julie says, "I always asked my children to take a thumb and press down the center of the cookie to add a little taste of love. This is what makes my peanut butter cookies taste so good–a little touch of love."

Bake at 350 degrees for about 12 minutes on lightly greased baking sheets.

Aunt Julie's Peanut Butter Cake

The standard birthday cake in the Helms' family is the Peanut Butter cake which is a Spice cake covered lavishly with peanut butter icing.

You will need the following ingredients:

A Spice cake (I do not know which brand she uses)

¾ cup of creamy peanut butter

3 cups sugar

1 ½ cup milk

Directions:

Bake a Spice cake following the recipe on the box.

For the frosting:

Stir milk and sugar over a low to medium heat.

Let it boil.

Stir.

At the first hint of the soft ball stage, take it off the burner.

Add ¾ cups of creamy peanut butter.

Julie says, "I pour it into a bowl because the pan holds the heat for too long. Beat it. When the icing is still warm I spoon it onto my cake layers. On that first layer I get about as close as a half inch from the edge of the layer. Add the next layer. Add the icing. Ice the sides. It's not always pretty, but it's always good."

She is right. Peanut Butter Cake is always good. I have tried to make the cake twice—it was never pretty, but it was delicious!

Beloved,

After Aunt Julie talked me through the steps of making the peanut butter icing the last time she said this:

"The next time you come to my house, I want you to call me when you are about a half hour away. When you walk in the door I am going to have warm cinnamon bread on the counter. Here's how we are going to eat the cinnamon bread. You will eat half a loaf, and I will eat the other half."

"What's the recipe for the cinnamon bread?" I asked, logically.

"It's going with me to my grave. Jody says I have to hold onto this one—no one else can have it."

"Why?"

"I don't know. That's just the way it is going to be."

Recipes are so good sometimes that we want the people we love best to enjoy them only with us. That's why Jody wants her to keep the recipe, so I will go and see them. They are both crazy about me. And I am crazy about them. That's why I had banana pudding steaming on the kitchen counter when Julie came to visit last time. Sometimes that waiting dish made just for visitors is part of the hug you give them when they first arrive.

I will go and visit them as soon as life allows, and we will eat that cinnamon bread. In time, Julie will tell me the recipe. But when she does, it will be because she has discovered some other special dish to make that she can use to coax me to visit her. And I will go—and not primarily for the recipe.

In the meantime, here's the recipe that your grandmother used to woo all of us to her house.

Lola's Sweet Potato Pie

Beloved,

In order to fully appreciate this pie, you need to know its history.

Your grandmother made these pies twice a year. The first time was near Thanksgiving but not on the day, and the next time was near Christmas but not on the day.

The day was always cool, and it never rained on Sweet Potato Pie Day.

The phone call that the pies were ready came out of the blue and, like firemen answering the call, anyone who was summoned dropped whatever she was doing and went to your grandmother's house and saw about a dozen or so pies lining the kitchen counters.

"Lunch," she announced.

And then we all ate sweet potato pie and only pie for lunch.

We didn't use plates.

The filling was so firm that she would hand you a slice on a napkin, and you held it like a sandwich. It was usually still warm. It was always good.

And then after lunch, your grandmother handed out the remaining warm, whole pies so that we all took home at least one for supper.

This pie is for sharing. And when your grandmother died suddenly, it took us a year or two to realize that no one in the family had the recipe.

That sent a number of us on a mission to figure out that recipe. We downloaded multiple recipes for sweet potato pie. We tried different recipes—lots of them actually. No recipe found on the Internet came close to creating the taste of home associated with your grandmother's pie—until I sat before God in prayer; and in the spirit of George Washington Carver, I prayed for a revelation. I explained it to God this way, and he heard me: "Mother's recipe wouldn't have been complicated. She never bought special ingredients to make the pie. She seemed to always have the ingredients. (This was true of many women of her generation because she didn't drive; and so unlike the often under-stocked pantries of women who can drive and go get anything that is needed or wanted, Mother usually had what she could envision needing stocked in her pantry.)

Finally, after making what I call my George Washington Carver prayer which was marinated with the faith that I had known the cook and I knew what was in her pantry, I sat down and wrote out a recipe that is as close to being hers as I can get this side of heaven. It is not exactly as good as hers, but the reason is not that the recipe is wrong. It is simply that the pie tasted better when I was with her and daddy and all of my family.

Now the pie stands alone with the memories, and they are good memories.

Here's what you need:

A good crust—(Your grandmother used a frozen crust. I don't.)

A 16 oz. can of sweet potatoes, simmered, drained, and mashed

Some brown sugar—Keep the box of sugar handy and add more if you want it.

Three eggs

A small can of evaporated milk

A teaspoon of vanilla extract

1 teaspoon of nutmeg

½ teaspoon of cinnamon

That's the pie right there.

Directions:

Beat the eggs. Add the simmered, drained, mashed sweet potatoes. Add the brown sugar—about third to a half of a box. Suit yourself. Add the spices. Add the milk. Add the vanilla extract. Beat on low with your mixer until creamy. Pour the soupy mixture into a pie crust that you have pierced multiple times with a fork so that the crust won't rise up into the pie.

Cook the pie at about 350 until the center is done. In my oven that's about forty-five minutes on the top shelf.

Eat warm for lunch with a friend you have called to come over and eat pie. Give the recipe freely to anyone who wants it.

Your grandmother would have shared the recipe if anyone had thought to ask her. I know this because of the Magic Focus mirror she gave me that I have in my desk drawer.

One day your grandmother saw a compact with a Magic Focus mirror, and suddenly your dear, nearsighted grandmother could see clearly to pluck her eyebrows again. She bought it from the drugstore and ordered a case of these compacts with the Magic Focus mirrors and gave them away to all of her friends and children. I have mine and hers.

That Magic Focus compact is a pretty good way to remember your grandmother—look at yourself clearly in a glass that reveals the truth and don't be afraid to share that same view of the world with others.

Your grandmother didn't mean to take the recipe for Sweet Potato Pie to her grave. It just happened because none of us could imagine life without her, so we just never asked her for it.

I'm quite sure she would have given us that Sweet Potato Pie recipe if we had asked, and I am also sure that she knew that one of her daughters would have been able to replicate it by simply remembering who she was.

Aunt Daphne's Praline-Topped Sweet Potatoes

You can make all kinds of versions of this casserole, but I like this one. However, I still like the same recipe with marshmallows browned lightly on top instead of the praline topping.

To make the casserole, you need these ingredients:

A very big can of sweet potatoes, simmered until tender, drained, mashed

Some pecans

Some butter—a stick or so—it's up to you

Some brown sugar

Directions:

Simmer the potatoes. Drain most of the syrup once they are tender. Pour the potatoes into a big mixing bowl because when you whip them, they splatter. Add some butter and brown sugar to taste—a half cup or so. You don't need them very sweet because the topping is sweet.

Once the potatoes and butter and sugar are whipped, spoon the mixture into a Pyrex dish and smooth it out to prepare the surface for your topping.

I use about a stick of butter and let it reach room temperature or microwave it in a mixing bowl for about fifteen seconds. You don't want the butter completely melted—just soft enough to work with. Add lots of brown sugar until you make a crumbly mixture. Add as many pecan pieces as you want to use.

Spoon this in dollops onto the top of the potatoes. It will spread out as it cooks.

Place the dish in your oven under the broiler and do not leave the oven. Watch it second by second until it begins to boil. Take the dish out immediately. When the potatoes cool, that topping hardens into praline crunchiness.

It's quite good.

Baked Chicken

What you need:

A nice fat chicken

The top rack of your oven moved lower so that the bird will fit inside your oven

Salt and pepper (I have a recipe for all kinds of spices that makes it a spicy bird, and if you ever want that recipe, call me.)

Directions:

Wash your whole chicken. Clean out whatever may have been stored inside the chicken. Unless you are planning to make some kind of gravy with those unattractive innards, just throw them away.

Place the chicken in a Pyrex dish sprayed with Pam. Salt and pepper. I sometimes add a bit of Cayenne Pepper for color and heat. Bake the bird uncovered on a low temperature—300 degrees or so—for 3-4 hours. If you need the chicken completely cooked before then, raise the temperature, but the increased heat will dry out the chicken. Baste the chicken when you notice enough liquid in the pan to spoon over the bird.

Serve with anything you like. I like couscous.

P.S. After washing the chicken, disinfect the sink, the sink handles, and any surface you touched.

BAKED TURKEY

What you need:

A clean countertop near the sink to work

A thawed-out turkey that has been rinsed inside and out

Some cooking oil to pat on the turkey's skin

A couple of stalks of celery

An onion

Salt and pepper

Directions:

Choose a turkey that has never been frozen when possible. If you like dark meat, choose the whole bird. If you prefer white meat, choose a turkey breast. If you are fretful about overcooking it, buy a turkey that has a built-in thermometer that pops out when the turkey is fully cooked. That device can be very reassuring.

Wash the turkey completely. (Disinfect the sink afterwards.)

Rub the turkey with cooking oil.

Stuff it with a couple of stalks of chopped celery and a chunked-up onion.

Salt and pepper it.

Cover with tin foil and cook on a low heat until the thermometer pops out. Then, take the tin foil off and cook uncovered until the skin browns and is crispy.

Use the drippings to make dressing and the gravy. I use about 75% for the dressing and the remaining liquid to make the gravy.

Cornbread Dressing

Ingredients you will need:

A large bag of cornbread mix (I keep about 5 pounds on hand and probably bake 2 lbs. for a 9 x 12 Pyrex dish)

Turkey drippings/broth

Chicken broth, too. (Usually I have a pint or two in my freezer)

Butter –a stick to sauté the onions and celery

Onions

Celery

Sage—a quarter of a cup or more

Milk

Eggs—enough to make the cornbread batter and another egg for the dressing

Salt and pepper

Optional: Pepperidge Farm Seasoned Bread Crumbs (about a third of a small bag for a large pan of dressing)

Kevin adds: "If you need to you can use poultry seasoning."

Directions:

Bake a big pan of cornbread early in the morning of the day you want to bake the turkey and dressing because your turkey will monopolize the oven later. You can eat a piece of this cornbread for lunch, and still have plenty for your dressing. I always do.

When the cornbread is cool, break it into squares, and then rub it piece by piece between your hands until it is finely crumbled. Add some Pepperidge Farm dressing dry mix if you want to add some flavor, but you don't need it. I don't use much—maybe a third of a small bag.

Add sage—lots of it. I use a lot of sage because I like the taste, but I don't use so much that it makes the dressing look green. A lot is something like a quarter to a half cup of sage depending upon how much dressing you make. I make enough dressing for three meals because I usually have enough meat for three meals—and that does not include the turkey sandwiches that I make, too.

While the finely-crumbled cornbread is melding with the sage you can sauté some celery and diced onions in a big skillet in a lot of butter. I use a stick. Then, pour the whole mixture over your crumbled cornbread. It adds flavor and liquid. You need all of it. The cornbread soaks it up!

Add salt and pepper.

Add chicken broth.

When the turkey is done, use most of the drippings from the turkey to add to your dressing but reserve some of that liquid to make your gravy if you want gravy with this dish. I use a portion of the turkey drippings to make a simple cream gravy. If you want a recipe for giblet gravy you will need to ask your Aunt Julie, who is the only person in the family who makes it (that I know of). I have never asked her because I do not want to make giblet gravy. (I do not know how to lay bricks because I do not want to lay a barbecue pit in the backyard, and I do not know how to play the organ because I do not want to be asked to play it at funerals.)

Stir the ingredients together well. There will be liquid brimming around the edges of your pan but you will see the dressing clearly—don't drown it. When it's time to place the dressing in the oven, take a big measuring cup and beat an egg in a cup of milk. Pour this eggy mixture over your cornbread dressing. This mixture will hold the dressing together. Cook for about 45 minutes to an hour depending on how hot your oven is. I cook mine at 350 degrees. It should be browned and crispy around the edges but still moist.

Homemade Cranberry Sauce

This recipe is one I got from Miss Esther, but it's mine now. To make cranberry sauce, you need a bag of cranberries and a wooden spoon and a tallish, heavy-bottomed sauce pan and some sugar.

Ingredients:

1 bag of beautiful cranberries (you can buy multiple bags on sale at Thanksgiving and freeze them and use them throughout the year for a little taste of the holidays anytime)

2 cups of sugar

1 cup of water

Directions:

Heat the water and sugar slowly until it makes a simple syrup. Then add the washed and picked over cranberries. Raise the temperature slowly, stirring. Using that wooden spoon crush the cranberries that do not pop naturally from the heat. Your intention is to bring this to a heat that is a little below soft ball stage. To know when this is right, watch the water boil slowly away and the mixture thicken on the side of your wooden spoon when you stir. When the sauce is holding onto the spoon well, take it off the heat and let it set a spell. Tidy up your kitchen. Then, spoon the sauce into a cool glass bowl and set it aside to reach room temperature. Cover the bowl and refrigerate.

Coca Cola Jell-O

Made at Christmastime mainly, this Jell-O salad can be as small or as big as you need it to be.

For two people you would need:

One small box of black cherry Jell-O

A small jar of drained and sliced cherries

A cup of chopped pecans

A small chilled Coke

Directions:

Follow the recipe for using the hot water to dissolve the Jell-O. Instead of cold water, use cold Coca-Cola.

Place in refrigerator until it has semi-set. Then, stir in the cherries and the nuts.

It's very pretty and works well as a dessert or as a side dish.

Beloved,

Here's an episode from our family life that will make you ask: "Where's that spinach dip recipe?" I don't have it. After this incident, I did not want it. You will see why shortly.

A Taste of Home....

Two Shakes of a Lamb's Tail

It was rib-eye steak night at my sister Mary Ellen's house, and I could tell before the Worcestershire sauce ever made it to me that Mama had something on her mind.

Finally, right after the baked potatoes had been passed out and the butter and sour cream were making the rounds, Mother cupped her hands formally in front of her as if to ask the blessing; but instead, she accused one of her daughters of being a bowl thief.

"I hate to have to say this. I really do," she began, sweeping our faces with that penetrating brown-eyed gaze. "But I have a deluxe Tupperware serving bowl with a snap lock lid, and I can't find it anywhere."

Daddy interrupted Mother. "There'll be no questions asked," he assured us. "I'm sure one of you girls just borrowed the bowl and forgot to tell your mother. But, she's going on a trip with her girlfriends next week, and she needs her bowl."

"They know I am responsible for bringing the spinach dip," Mother said, and her tone was less prayerful.

This offense committed against her was more than simple theft. Her honor as the spinach dip queen was in question if she did not have the perfect bowl to carry it in, and the fact that one of her own children would put her reputation in such jeopardy was on par in her mind with what King Lear's viperish girls did to their parent.

The room fell silent as we supposedly contemplated our consciences, but this awkward silence was soon broken by my nephew, Matthew, who obviously sympathized with mother's plight but did not understand the implications inherent in the alleged crime. He only knew that someone else had lost something, and he had, too.

"Talk about things disappearing," Matthew said. "I cannot find my sheep's tail. I have looked all over the backyard for it.

Matthew belongs to the Future Farmers of America and is raising a sheep as a project.

"I thought you wanted your sheep's tail to fall off," Dad remarked. "What was it I heard about your putting that special rubber band on the tail to cut off the circulation so that it would fall off?"

Matthew nodded yes, vigorously. "That's right. I did that. You remember."

He is young and does not yet understand that remembering something before it disappeared is not the same thing as coming up with a clue that will aid in finding it.

I felt sorry for Matt, so I added a two-cent memory. "I saw your sheep and his tail a few days ago. That tail was hanging straight down the back of your animal, and it didn't sway one iota. It looked like a dead tail to me."

"The tail is supposed to die and fall off. And it should be out in the back yard somewhere, but I can't find it."

"Your sheep probably buried his tail after it fell off. You will never find it," Mother said, impatiently dismissing her grandson's problem. She was intent on solving her own. "What I want to know is, where is my spinach dip bowl?"

None of us would look Mother in the eye when she asked that question. I don't know why my sisters couldn't face her, but I could not look at Mother because my biscuit-making bowl has been missing for a long time, and I figured that she might have it. I'm loath to accuse my mother or any of my sisters of being a bowl thief, because I was raised to believe that stealing a woman's favorite bowl is akin to borrowing her last pair of designer panty hose without permission or using her lipstick that she has just managed to make match the shape of her lips.

"I just think it's curious that one day I have something and the next day I don't," Mother summed up bitterly.

At last, she picked up her steak knife and began to saw through her piece of meat. It was cold, and the cutting was tough work. Determined, she kept at it. By then, none of us had much of an appetite, and we fiddled with our salads.

Something in Mother's tone triggered a gallant impulse in Dad, who stopped altogether being our protective father, and once again assumed his position as Mother's hero.

"This reminds me of those days when all of you girls still lived at home, and I could never find my scissors or my Scotch tape or the glue. When I asked any of you where something was no one had ever seen it." Just remembering the good old days made Dad bitter. "Those things didn't just walk off by themselves, and neither did your mother's bowl."

"There is another solution to the mystery of things disappearing," I offered tentatively. "Is it possible that one of us has multiple-personality disorder?"

They didn't know what I meant at first, so I explained. "I am reading this book where the main character gets kidnapped as a little girl and is abused and because the stress is so awful, her personality splits off into different people. Later in life, one of those split-off parts of her gets accused of murdering her English teacher, and her own sister thinks she could have done it. The girl can't defend herself because she has no conscious memory of what the other personalities do."

"I thought when you outgrew Nancy Drew we wouldn't have to listen to any more plot summaries from books at the dinner table," my oldest sister complained. She was the hostess for our family supper, and it wasn't going well. She had decided to blame me.

"None of you girls was ever kidnapped," Mother interjected, sounding regretful. "Furthermore, none of my girls would dare to have multiple personalities. I wouldn't permit that. One personality is enough for any well-bred person."

"The only reason I am bringing this up is that the other day I was trying to gather my income tax information, and I went to find my record of contributions to the church where I know I put it, and my tax document was gone."

"That happens to me every year," Dad said. "I call myself putting all the receipts in one place; but when I go to look for them, they are not all there." His gaze swept us again—a foreign look in his eye that didn't seem like our daddy at all.

"I don't guess it's likely that two people in the same family would have multiple personality disorder," I conceded. "There must be another explanation." I studied my sisters to see if I could tell whether they were hiding some other kinds of mischievous, secret women behind their eyes.

Reading my mind, they faced me unashamed, unafraid of what I might see.

Actually, I was the first to look away.

When I did, my nephew announced, looking right at me: "There's your bowl thief right there."

"I did not take my mother's bowl," I denied, shocked by my nephew's accusation. "I have my own bowls. I have two Tupperware bowls with snap lock lids of my own. I don't need to steal anyone's bowl."

"What color are your bowls?" Mother asked softly. Her brown-eyed gaze pierced me.

"What color was yours?" I asked, drawing back.

"You first," she ordered.

"One bowl is red, and the other bowl is yellow."

She chewed a small bite of steak slowly, then swallowed. "My bowl is yellow. When did you buy your so-called yellow bowl?"

I had no memory of making the purchase, and I could not explain why I would have bought two bowls of different colors.

The silence was unbearable. I broke it. "The yellow Tupperware bowl is mine, but you are welcome to have it."

"I guess I am," Mother said, settling back.

"See there," Daddy said. "I told you we'd find your bowl."

I could feel some inner part of my personality attempting to split off as I was falsely accused of a crime I had not committed. My own mother was stealing my bowl, and my father was backing her up.

While my family drifted into a lighter conversation, I, abused, maligned, robbed of my yellow bowl and my biscuit bowl, took the higher road of martyred silence and, holding tightly onto my identity by keeping a firm grip on my knife and fork, resolved to finish my dinner nobly, heroically, as if I had nothing to hide.

This course of action was not easy, considering the intense, accusing, as yet unasked questions about a missing sheep's tail still lurking in my young nephew's innocent eyes.

Section 3
The Egg and I and You

What's in this section:

Meringue

Lemon Meringue Pie

Cousin Kevin's Divinity

Egg Salad Sandwiches

Egg and Sausage Casserole

A Taste of Home: *A Dog Story*

CRACKING THE EGG....

You will crack countless eggs in your lifetime, and you will, over time, have your own associations with the incredible egg, for it can transform from one substance to another in a way that only water does when it can also boil and then become an ice cube (that expands, which is contrary to how one typically and intuitively thinks about freezing).

Eggs can do that. They can separate and expand.

There are occasions in your life when you will need to separate the yolk from the egg white. Everyone eventually figures out the best method for this. It is a matter of balance and, ultimately, how much goo you can stand on your fingertips for any length of time. For me, the two big tricks are not to catch part of the yellow yolk with a shard from the egg shell and let it contaminate the white which is what you usually need: pure unsullied egg whites in order to make something like meringue. Or Angel Food Cake. Or egg white omelets which you craved after you had your tonsils out.

When I need only the whites of an egg or the yolk itself, I tap my egg on the side of a bowl that has a lip so that the break is clean. Then, holding two halves of the egg shell in each hand I tip the yolk back and forth between the two sides while the egg white slips down the side of the shell into a bowl reserved to catch the egg whites. If one side of the egg shell is smaller and holds the yolk closer, you will get a much better separation of the white from the yolk, but this really is about practice and your own tolerance for how much egg white you are willing to let fall. (Know, too, that some egg producers create a better-quality shell by feeding their chickens better. Consistently, Costco's eggs are better than the ones I can buy in any local grocery store.)

After you have the egg white in one bowl and the yolk in another, you must look around for a dog to give the yolk to because it is a sin to pour a perfectly good egg yolk down the drain. In our family there have always been dogs, and when a recipe called for the number of egg whites and separated yolks that matched exactly the number of dogs in the family it was considered a very good recipe. When I separated an egg, Tarzan got the yolk.

In spite of all the dogs that we fed yolks to over the years, the number one dog in the family that you did not know was a German shepherd named Tarzan. His best friend was another German shepherd that lived next door whose name was Mr. Mooney. They were pals, and if it was a two-egg yolk recipe day, then Mr. Mooney received the other yolk. He would come if you called him and gulp down an egg yolk just as if he were our very own dog.

But Tarzan got the first yolk, and he always received a benediction from your grandmother when she was giving it to him: "Here, Boy, this will add a sheen to your coat." Mother, someone who trained to be a hairdresser like you, believed in cultivating a shiny coat for Tarzan, and I will tell you with some assurance that when she fed us eggs, I could see her checking the sheen of our hair to see if we were being underfed a protein that she devoutly believed was a secret to beauty for girls and dogs alike, and there was no real differentiation between the dog's shiny coat or the girls' gleaming hair. Family pride all around was family pride.

But, Tarzan was universally the pride of the family, and it was because of a singular day when your Aunt Julie at the very young age of six or so wondered out of the house on Edgemont Avenue and down the street where, espying a street culvert, she went exploring and got stuck in that culvert. Tarzan was with her. Julie's cries for help went unheard because she was small and her voice faint at the time, but Tarzan barked loudly. And barked. And barked.

Shiny coat and all, Tarzan barked until those of us who went looking for Julie heard her and found him standing guard by the culvert from which your Aunt Julie was extricated, clasped, cherished, wept over, and as each hand reached out to touch her, the other hand reached out to pat the head of the dog that had summoned help and stood guard until help arrived. (Actually, help other than us arrived first, but not knowing the strangers, Tarzan barked them away from his favorite Julie until the people he recognized as the givers of the egg yolks and head pats appeared, and only then did the protector of Julie step aside and allow the baby in the family to be rescued.)

So, when I separate eggs I think of Tarzan and of the other dogs and of your grandmother and of you, now, a hair stylist, and I wonder if you ever tell your clients to eat more eggs to make their hair shiny. If you ever have that impulse, you came by it naturally for stories like that pass down through a family as discreetly as pats on the head occur throughout a lifetime, and now, for some of the pats on your head and the eggs you have been fed, you know the story of Tarzan and Julie in the culvert and how a simple egg being cracked has become part of that story for me when I cook.

When I make meringue for one pie I use three egg whites and three dogs get a yolk each, but if there are no dogs—and there are no dogs right now—then I make a banana pudding if I have bananas and a lemon pie if I have lemons. It truly grieves me to throw out egg yolks.

MERINGUE

You will need for one pie:

Sugar—you will add this by teaspoon as you work

A hint of vanilla extract

A clean glass bowl

A good mixer

You will need 3 egg whites to make the kind of meringue that raises the eye brows and appetites of others or two if you are don't care about showing off.

Often that recipe for a meringue will call for Cream of Tartar. Even though I have Cream of Tartar in my pantry, I have never seen a difference between meringue made with it and meringue made without it, so I don't use Cream of Tartar, but when a neighbor needs some and comes to borrow mine I am always very smug about having plenty on hand.

Directions:

Get your egg whites ready in a glass bowl that can handle the height of the meringue as it grows.

Starting slowly, beat the egg whites until they become foamy.

Add teaspoons of sugar and keep beating.

Add more sugar in small amounts. I don't measure the sugar. I add and taste.

Some recipes call for a splash of vanilla extract—I like it, but it will darken your meringue so just a hint is all you want.

Beat until the egg whites are stiff and form a peak in the bowl. Ever taken a bubble bath and had the bubbles so stiff that you could push them into shapes? When your meringue does that, it's ready. Spread it on a pie or a pudding. It is very good on banana pudding though you will find that most people use some artificial whipped topping.

Pudding with real meringue is better.

Then, whatever you have put your meringue on goes in the oven for just a few minutes—maybe five plus minutes—until the top is only slighted tanned (not brown).

Bring out the dish to cool.

Later, after the pie or pudding has been served and there are left-overs, the meringue will develop drops of moisture. *Did you do something wrong?* No. Meringue has a short life span, so it is better to eat a dish made with meringue sooner than later.

Meringue is especially good on Lemon Meringue pie, and it is a reasonable dish to make because the lemon filling of this pie calls for the yolks that were separated from the egg whites. But then you do not get to give one to a dog, and there is often a feeling of regret about that.

I was the resident Lemon Meringue pie maker in the family growing up, but I don't make them anymore. There aren't any people who used to like them around to eat them now. However, all you need to know about Lemon Meringue pie is that a cooked filling is better than a store-bought one or that awful stuff that comes in a can. Don't buy that and don't use it.

Here's my recipe for the lemon filling for a pie:

Lemon Meringue Pie

Ingredients

1 ½ cups sugar

⅓ cup cornstarch

1 ½ cups sugar

3 beaten egg yolks

2 tablespoons butter

½ cup of fresh lemon juice

1 cup water

Zest of one lemon

A prepared pie shell

Directions:

Mix sugar, cornstarch, lemon juice and water on stove.

Boil one minute. Add half to egg yolks. Then, add the rest. Boil one more minute. Add the rest of the ingredients.

Pour into prepared, baked pie shell.

Top with meringue.

Beloved,

In the discussion of Lemon Meringue Pie, you will most certainly come to the important question of which kind of pie shell to use. I prefer a graham cracker crust pie shell because the tang of the graham cracker and the crunch goes well with the soft filling, but I am often alone in that perspective.

Others enjoy the regular pie shell, and I always think they are wrong and lack imagination, but I could be wrong and lack imagination myself, so there you are.

The divinity of egg whites....

There are other ways to use egg whites, and one of those ways is to make Divinity candy, which most people seem to want at Christmas. I have always thought that Divinity candy would be perfect at weddings, but in all my born and born-again days, I have never seen it used like that.

It is one of the candies that people associate with needing a cool, dry day if the recipe is to succeed, but you will have to ask your cousin Kevin about that. Divinity candy, like Red Velvet Cake, is one of Kevin's signature dishes.

Inside a family, people have signature dishes, and when this becomes very true over time (and the person who makes it is not self-deluded– and some are) then the family steps aside and lets that family member be the one who brings that dish to family suppers and other kinds of gatherings. Beware of this largesse because sometimes it does not mean that the person can cook that dish well. It can also mean that it is the only dish you cook well enough that others can stand to eat.

Like church, where different cooks have signature dishes that they can be counted on to bring, our family counts on Kevin to make the Divinity, and it is very good.

Cousin Kevin's Divinity

"Just remember 8 minutes. Remember 8 minutes from the time it starts to boil, and it will turn out fine."

What you need:

½ cup white Karo syrup

½ cup water

⅛ teaspoon salt

Two cups of sugar

Two egg whites

1 teaspoon of vanilla extract

Nuts (optional)

Directions:

Separate your egg whites and place them in a big metal or plastic bowl. Let them sit until they reach room temperature. In a two-quart, thick-bottomed saucepan, combine:

½ cup of white Karo syrup

½ cup water

⅛ teaspoon salt

Stir.

Add two cups of sugar.

Stirring over a medium heat, bring the mixture slowly to a high heat and a boil.

When the mixture reaches a boil, reduce the heat to medium and start the count of 8 minutes.

When you can take a spoon and drip some of the liquid and it creates a fine thread, it's done. There will be no smell. If you can smell it, it's overcooked.

Remove from the heat. Add the vanilla extract while it's still hot. Add it slowly or it will boil over.

Then, let that mixture rest while you beat the egg whites and add ½ cup sugar to stiffen the egg whites.

When they have reached their peak, while holding the mixer, slowly drizzle the hot liquid through the fast-moving beaters into the egg whites. Beat until it's cool to form puffs of divinity. The consistency will be like marshmallow cream.

Add nuts if you like nuts. But use a good nut. Good nuts are worth the extra money, and if you buy locally, you support your farming community.

Drop by large spoonsful onto waxed paper.

Share with friends.

Egg Salad or Egg Salad Sandwiches

Sometimes you run out of luncheon meat and don't want to go out to lunch. Often, you will still have plenty of eggs, and you can make egg salad. For each person, boil two eggs until hard (about five minutes once the water is roiling).

What you need:

Hard-boiled eggs (2-3 a person)

Mayonnaise

Relish

Salt and pepper

Directions:

Peel the eggs and chop into a mixing bowl. Salt and pepper. Add mayonnaise and sweet relish. Be careful with the relish. Drain the liquid or it will make your egg salad too soupy. You want a firm egg salad. Serve it with crackers or on bread as an egg salad sandwich.

Egg and Sausage Casserole

Ingredients:

6 slices or so of bread, cubed (I freeze half loaves of bread when they are getting stale and pull them out and thaw them for this kind of dish and for making French toast.)

1 pound sausage, browned, drained

1 ½ cups shredded Cheddar cheese

8 eggs, beaten

2 cups milk

Salt and pepper to suit yourself.

Directions:

Cube the slices of bread and place in greased 9 x13 pan or baking dish. Top with sausage and cheese. Mix eggs, milk, salt and pepper. Pour over ingredients in pan. You can cover and chill overnight. If left overnight, remove from refrigerator and bring to room temperature before baking.

Bake 45 minutes at 325 degrees or until set.

P. S. You will see this dish show up at Sunday school breakfasts, and people who are truly ready to meet their Maker will eat it even when it's cold. (I don't.)

The egg's story can never be finished being told completely, Beloved, but I will leave you with this story from the Betty Crocker company. Originally a flour-producing company, the Betty Crocker company developed flour mixes, like Bisquick (get some right away—it's incredibly versatile) and cake mixes.

As our country grew up, Betty Crocker did, too, and the product lines from that company paralleled the evolution of our country's economy and met its eating and budget needs through the Depression of 1929 and later through two world wars when certain ingredients were hard to find.

There was no real Betty Crocker, but an actress spoke for her; and in the early days, Betty Crocker was on the radio where she taught cooking over the air and answered questions about cooking—questions that often veered to a discussion of love.

Questions like these occur because love and food are so closely intertwined:

Q: "Can the lady next door steal my man if she cooks a better chocolate cake than mine?"

A: "No, but to be on the safe side, here's a great recipe for chocolate cake," replied the actress playing Betty Crocker.

Beloved,

These letters to Betty that were answered over the air created a bond between consumers, cooks and the Betty Crocker company. The company remained profitable during some very lean economic times in our country; and when America was polled to see who was the most influential woman of her time, Betty Crocker came in second behind Eleanor Roosevelt.

But here's one more piece of information about the egg and cooking you might need to know. There was a time during the rationing of goods in our country when the Betty Crocker people decided to produce a cake mix with a dried egg in it. While their other mixes had sold well, this cake mix did not.

When they investigated, the executives discovered that even the few cooks using the mix with the dried eggs felt as if they were not putting enough of themselves in a cake that was meant to represent their love for their family—or their man.

When the company concluded that this was the reason the mix was not selling, they took out the dried egg and added the new instructions on the box: Add two fresh eggs. The cake mixes sold well after that because there is something innate in us that makes us want to give more of ourselves when we cook and during that time in history the egg was that symbol.

A Taste of Home....

A Dog Story

The peacocks next door killed themselves accidentally, flying up into the roof of their enclosure because, says the neighbor who owned the birds, my father's dogs barked at them.

Taking that neighbor's word for it that peacocks cannot stand dogs barking, Dad reimbursed the man for the dead birds and had an electric fence installed to keep his dogs respectful of their neighbors.

This neighbor took Dad's money, promptly gave up raising peacocks; and then, much to my father's amazement, he bought a fancy, blue-haired dog. The kind of dog, the neighbor says, that does not bark: "I've trained my dog not to bark, and he never does."

That man's boast is an outright lie. His dog always barks a blue streak at me, but it's nothing compared with some of the other neighbor trouble we've had.

Because our Dad does not like to chain up Luke, his Labrador, for a while he would let the dog race along through the neighborhood beside his car. Though Dad and Luke enjoyed the thrill of this competition, the race angered some of the neighbors.

My nephew Matt reported, "The lady down the street said that if Dad ever runs over her Chihuahua while he's racing Luke, she's gonna sue him for a million dollars."

"I've come to a complete stop to let that Chihuahua cross the street," my father said in self-defense.

"That's not all," Matt added. "I hear that the policeman you sold that house to is waiting for you with the radar gun, Pa, and he's gonna catch you racing Luke and give you a speeding ticket."

"Forewarned is forearmed," Dad commented, tight-lipped.

"I told you not to sell that house to those people," Mother said.

Dad pays scant attention to Mother's intuition. He sometimes also ignores the so-called facts. He had helped the policeman get financing for his home. But he knew the cop had had some heavy medical bills recently, so he chalked up the speeding ticket comment to strain.

Dad's the sort of person who thinks, 'If I were in that kind of shape, I'd sure like someone to help me.' He doesn't understand that people who accept help sometimes resent their benefactors.

He certainly can't fathom the attitude of the former peacock owner, who told Matt he wants to watch Dad get that speeding ticket.

Dad can't accept the fact that there is no pleasing some people. My mother understands. Good neighbors learn this lesson the hard way.

Now Dad ties up Luke whenever he leaves the house. He grieves, "I don't know why anyone would want to see me in particular get a speeding ticket."

There is one reason. I know Dad tries to be a good neighbor, but he is also infamous in the neighborhood as a dognapper. Lady, Spot, Big Shot and The Incredible Hulk all left neighborhood owners over a period of nine months to move in with Dad because he fed them during the day while their owners were at work, and they followed him home and stayed for the grub. Neighbors who have experienced the public shame of being deserted by their pets have very long memories.

As a gesture of consolation, I bought Dad a T-shirt with the slogan, If You Can't Run With the Big Dogs You Better Stay on The Porch.

"Wear this shirt when you drive by that Chihuahua's house," I suggested.

Other than the daily conflicts of living next door to expiring peacocks and a barking non-barker and claiming kinship to a confirmed dognapper, my own days in this neighborhood have stayed pretty much the same. The neighbor's dog patrols the common fence that separates our properties. Whenever I pedal my bike past him on my way to the mailbox, he barks at me. I holler back, unashamed, "Shut up, you loud-mouthed, worrisome mutt!"

May heaven forgive me for taking my unneighborly anger out on that blue-blooded, show-off dog. But really, if I were a peacock, I'd be dead by now.

Section 4

The Onion, the Potato, and Being an Outlaw Cook

What's in this section:

Potato Soup

Suppertime Potato Salad

Homemade French Fries

Corned Beef Hash

Meatloaf

Cousin Kevin's Bacon-Fried Cabbage

A Taste of Home: *The Secret Language of Married Women*

To enjoy the onion best become an Outlaw Cook

There will be times in your life when you will have to be an Outlaw Cook. That means you will have a few ingredients in the house and no recipe that calls for exactly what you have. At least, that is what it means to me. (Toni Brooks, who used the expression in my presence, may mean something else entirely by it. I don't know. I stole the title from her, which makes me an Outlaw Writer and an Outlook Cook.)

But back to being an innovative cook, which is what I mean by the term.

It could be snowing outside.

You could not feel well.

You may not care what you eat, but you need to eat something. Not every meal is greatly important, but you may have to cook something anyway.

For this occasion you will need to become an Outlaw Cook. Break the rules. Use what you have. Serve it with confidence, and then nod confidently while you chew.

When the occasion of needing to be an Outlaw Cook arises, you will most likely have no meat in the house except in the freezer—and how quickly you lose an appetite for two hamburger patties that have been in there longer than you can remember and you meant to write the date with a black Sharpie on the foil packet but you couldn't find the pen that day and so you shoved the unmarked packet into the freezer and now you can't bear the idea of eating what's inside—so, you look around the kitchen and you have three onions and a few potatoes and inside the fridge is some cheese—doesn't matter what kind. Your grandmother swore by Colby. Your mother is a Parmesan girl. Your Aunt Julie likes all cheese and so does her husband Jody, and it is Jody who is the most inspiring person in the family to point to in the discussion of the single ingredient that all Outlaw Cooks depend upon: the onion.

Your Uncle Jody will take an onion, hollow out the middle, and fill it with some brown sauce he loves. Then he bakes it until tender and all the petals of the onion are flavored with his saucy elixir. He serves that onion with pride and encouragement to others to try some. Though he loves that onion himself, he is very generous with it. (Tip: Find a man whose instinct is to share generously what he himself loves best and you have found a man you can trust.)

I can't eat Jody's onion without having a gallbladder attack, so I do what you must always do when someone tries to encourage you to eat something that will kill you: Say no.

I am a modest eater of onions though I grew up eating them served sliced in apple cider vinegar for beans and rice night. Excellent! If you do not eat the onion, you can spoon some onion-flavored vinegar on your beans, and it's great.

I grew up seeing your grandparents eat fried egg and onion sandwiches, and, if my memory holds, these are famously referred to in an old movie called "Harvey."

I have heard that when you have a house to sell, you can place an onion on a cookie sheet and stick it in the oven. Turn the heat to low to fill the house with the smells of something good cooking. However, I do not think this is a good idea because that aroma is not everyone's idea of home cooking. (Cinnamon works better, I think, although there are people alive who do not like cinnamon.)

But back to using that onion on Outlaw Cook night.

If you have an onion and a few potatoes and some chicken broth or a couple of cubes of chicken bouillon you can make potato soup. Your mother has the recipe for this.

Here's your Aunt Julie's: (Mine is pretty much the same except I begin with chicken broth instead of water, and I like lots of garlic.)

Potato Soup is your friend on Outlaw Cook night, and you can make and serve it in just about any variation on the theme that you like.

Potato Soup

What you need:

A big cooking pot

6 or more nice-sized potatoes

Fresh garlic

Some milk—a cup or so (If I have Half & Half in the house, I use that.)

An onion

Some butter—suit yourself

Chicken bouillon or substitute for this sans MSG—check the label

Directions:

Fill the pot about halfway with water. You can add some chicken broth or use all broth. Use what you have.

Cook your peeled and chunked potatoes. I add about 3 or 4 cloves of peeled, mashed garlic. Place the potatoes and the garlic in the water and bring it to a boil.

When the potatoes are fork-tender, scoop out a cup of the broth. Add some milk to that and return the mixture to the soup. Stir.

Add butter—two or three tablespoons.

I serve potato soup with cornbread if I have an egg and enough milk. If not, it is Ritz crackers, which I like very much and consider to be an oft-forgotten cracker.

In addition to making potato soup, you can make a potato dish that is some kind of variation on scalloped potatoes and serve this as your entrée.

One night I had a bell pepper, a small onion, four potatoes, some Mozzarella cheese (I didn't use much because I don't digest dairy products easily now).

I peeled and sliced the washed potatoes into thin slices with finely diced peppers and onions and layered them in a Pyrex dish sprayed with Pam. I added a bit of water—about an inch. I added the cheese and a drizzle of milk. Then I baked it for about forty-five minutes until the top was browned. We ate it with appetite, believing that if I were to make *Potatoes Daphne* again I would add more onion. Fearing I would overpower the dish, I only used half the onion. I was wrong. I could have used the whole onion—maybe two.

But that is a matter of taste, Beloved.

The onion is your friend.

Cut it up very small for cornbread dressing and potato dishes. You can leave it out of potato salad. Your grandmother put it in, and I didn't like it. I make potato salad without onions, and I will often make it for supper and serve it warm.

Daphne's Suppertime Potato Salad

What you need:

As many potatoes as you think you need—six or so

Some mayonnaise

Yellow mustard (or some other kind—it's all good)

Cubed sweet pickles or sweet pickle relish

Salt and pepper

Directions:

Boil the peeled and cubed potatoes until fork tender

I use about six potatoes for two people when that is all we are going to eat.

Drain the water.

In a large bowl, use about a cup of mayonnaise, a quarter cup of yellow mustard (maybe more if you like that mustard taste), and a quarter cup of pickle relish. Get ready to add more of any of the above if this isn't enough to coat your potatoes. You won't know that until you stir it in and find out.

Coat the potatoes in the dressing and salt and pepper to taste. Some people add Cayenne pepper on the top for color, but potato salad doesn't need it. Serve warm. Then, refrigerate and serve the left-overs cold with anything. Cold potato salad gives you something to look forward to the next day.

Beloved,

While most people believe that chocolate and chocolate cake are the foods of love, they are underestimating the French Fried potato, which I came to recognize as the food of love back when your Aunt Mary Ellen was dating your Uncle Steve. He would come over on their date nights. They would sit on the long green sofa in the den, scanning channels until they found something to watch. It didn't matter who else was in the room; when Steve was there we watched what would suit him, and I don't remember what he liked to watch. I remember that while he was watching it, he was eating homemade French Fries made by his Beloved, your Aunt Mary Ellen. The rest of us got a sample of it—a couple of hot fries—but the whole plate was for him to share with Mary Ellen, and they sat companionably on the couch, in love and happy with homemade French Fries, which make a mess to cook but are worth the effort.

Homemade French Fries

What you need:

Potatoes

Crisco Oil

A big dinner plate covered in a paper towel to drain the hot fries on

Some catsup

Salt

Something good to watch on TV

The den darkened, with a throw on the side of the couch so that you can cover the hand that you are holding, if the night is chilly

Directions:

In a skillet, pour enough grease to cover the potatoes once they are cut up in the size you like. Bring the grease up slowly to the temperature you need. Do not add the potatoes until the grease is ready; otherwise, they will be greasy. Mary Ellen made man-sized fries, which is a potato peeled and cut in lengths. Some restaurants call these Steak Fries. Were the lengths of the potatoes cut in fourths? Eighths? Who knows? Cut them to suit yourself. Get them golden brown. Salt well. Serve piled high on a plate with catsup on the side.

I think Levi will enjoy them. Steve did.

Corned Beef Hash

Ingredients:

Can of corned beef that you have in the pantry for the kind of night when you need to cook something and don't have any fresh meat or fish

One good-sized onion, diced

A third of a stick of real butter (I use a little more butter when I am making this with real potatoes because it adds flavor to the potatoes, which are heartier than canned potatoes.)

About six potatoes, peeled and sliced. The size of slice you use depends on how much time you have to cook the dish. If you are in a hurry, slice the potato about the same thickness as you would a banana over your cereal. And, yes, you can use canned potatoes (drained), and sometimes I do when I don't have any fresh potatoes in the house. They're not as good, but don't expect as good a taste as fresh and you won't be disappointed.

Directions:

Sauté the onions in the butter.

Add the meat.

Add the potatoes.

Add water to cover the potatoes.

Make the cornbread. It takes the real potatoes longer to cook than the canned ones, so you can dawdle with the cornbread. If you have the ingredients you could even make a peach cobbler to go with this because if you reduce the heat of your oven to 400-375 you can slide that cobbler in beside the cornbread.

Aunt Daphne's Meatloaf

What you need:

Start with a pound or so of good-quality ground beef (I choose ground sirloin if it is on sale) if you are cooking for two.

A tube of fresh Saltines

The juice of a sweet onion

1-2 eggs, depending on how much meat you are using

Catsup

Worcestershire sauce

Salt and pepper

A disposable glove, if you don't think you can stand to touch the raw meat

Directions:

Crunch up a handful of Saltine crackers—add more if that doesn't look like enough for you.

Add a whole egg (or two).

Some people add a very small can of tomato paste. I used to but I don't any more. I like it better without it.

You can add some Worcestershire sauce if you like that taste. I do. Add as much as you want and don't let other people tell you how much that should be. With meatloaf, you are the boss.

Add the juice of one onion.

Salt and pepper this mixture and work the crackers, egg and onion juice into the meat with one well-washed hand. You can wear a vinyl, disposable glove if the sensation of all that stuff on your skin bothers you. It doesn't bother me.

Spray a Pyrex baking dish with Pam or something like that spray and mold your meatloaf into a flattened loaf. I cook mine wide and flat, so that I am assured that it is done all the way through. It slices better, too.

Drizzle some catsup across the top. Your cousin Kevin uses a jar of Ragu garden vegetable spaghetti sauce on his, but that's too red for me. I just use the catsup.

Then, I bake the dish uncovered it until it gets very singed around the edges.

Serve this with potato salad, creamed potatoes, or Cousin Kevin's Fried Cabbage.

Cousin Kevin's Fried Cabbage

What you need:

A head of cabbage

4-6 slices of bacon

A good-sized pan

Directions:

Fry 4-6 slices of bacon. Remove the bacon.

Chunk up a washed head of cabbage and situate it into a large sauce pan. Spoon the bacon grease over it. Add a little water to create a bath that will steam. Cover the pan and simmer for about twenty minutes until the cabbage is wilted. Crumble the bacon onto it.

Salt and pepper to taste.

Beloved,

Through history the onion has been a staple. It was used in Olympia to train athletes to compete. They ate onions, drank onion juice, and rubbed onions on their skin.

In the Middle Ages, the onion was a staple and often used as currency to pay the rent and to offer as a wedding gift.

Respect the onion, and let its audacity and potential inspire you to be an Outlaw Cook when the occasion and your pantry demand that you answer the question "What's for supper?" with creativity. Learn to listen that way, too. There are all kinds of conversations that happen in and outside a marriage. In the beginning, freshly-married people start out proclaiming their love for one another very passionately. But over time, they can sound like this. It is still the language of love. Learn to hear between the lines.

The Sounds of Home...

The Secret Language of Married Women

"I got my husband straightened out again," my hairdresser admitted. She wasn't talking to me. She was talking to a long-time married friend who had dropped by the hair salon to visit. I live in a small town where this is normal behavior.

I was marinating under a plastic cap getting a new hair color, awaiting my next step in the beauty process, and she had temporarily tuned out my presence.

"He was giving me a hard time this weekend about not having enough togetherness time, and so I told him, `All right, you want togetherness, I'll give you togetherness.' Well, I didn't let him go to the bathroom by himself for two days."

"Sometimes it takes that," her friend admitted. "They just get sooooo possessive."

"I can be standing in my housecoat and slippers, and he wants to know where I'm going, like he thinks I'm going farther than the mailbox in my housecoat."

"I don't know what it is about men. Some men just have to watch you all the time, like they think you're going to disappear all of a sudden."

"Been married seventeen years. I'm really gonna disappear."

"Some men don't trust time. What do you think got him started this time?"

"Oh, he's jealous of that horse I bought. He actually thought I was going to keep that horse at our house and ride it around the backyard."

"No one keeps a horse at the house in the city."

"You know that, and I know that, but my loving husband thought we were going to keep a horse in our backyard. I guess he could picture me riding the horse down to the mailbox and back again in my housecoat—like that was going to satisfy me."

"You wouldn't be satisfied," her friend agreed softly.

The woman with the new horse paused, as if she thought her friend meant something else, decided she didn't, and continued with her horse tale.

"Anyway, I keep the horse over at Daddy's place, just like a normal person would, and when my darling found that out he started the speech that begins `You're always leaving me. You don't want to be with me anymore.' So, naturally, I told him, `I do too want to be with you. You can come and watch me ride the horse,' But he won't ever. He's afraid that someone will dare him to get on a horse, and he will have to do it."

"That's all in his mind."

"Everything is. Anyway, I told him that I was going to ride the horse this afternoon when I got off from work and that he would have to learn to like it. I need to go some places!" She announced exasperated.

"That was a mistake," her friend commented.

"Anything I said would have been. The only way to please a man when he gets in this mood is to stay home all the time."

"My husband used to want me to stay home all the time, but I go so much now, he doesn't even ask me where I've been when I get back." She said the words proudly, but there was some regret there, too.

I heard it. Her friend didn't.

"When I left the house this morning, my husband actually stood in the doorway and said, `I think I'm going to buy a horse. We could go riding together.'"

"That's crazy. He isn't ever going to get on a horse."

"I know that, and you know that."

They both looked at me suddenly to see if I knew that, too.

Why do married women think that single women don't understand the checks and balances of married life? That we can't understand the language of togetherness? I bet when her husband asks, "Where are you going?" he means: 'I want some attention from you, but I don't want to ask for it directly.' And when the good wife reports that she got her husband straightened out, she really means she gave her darling the attention he wanted, but she didn't want her girlfriend to think that her husband was winning in this no-need-to-win battle between the sexes. And when she said, "He thinks I'm going to disappear," she really means, 'I love him terrible and he loves me terrible, and it's such a fierce business that I can't believe it's only been 17 years since our love began.'

This was actually a pretty sweet love story unfolding in front of me, and I was just about to get a little misty-eyed when the good wife continued: "So I asked him, `What in the world are you going to do with a horse of your own—watch it to death?'"

Section 5

Flour, Gravy, and Gallbladders

What's in this section:

Lola's Southern Woman Gravy

Aunt Mary Ellen's Gravy

Aunt Guin's Cream Gravy

Country Fried Steak

A Taste Of Home: *That Missing Piece of Nora's Cake*

Apricot Nectar Cake

Gravy and Gallbladders

You haven't heard the word gallbladder much, but a number of members of our immediate family have had their gallbladders removed.

Your grandmother did, too. So did your assorted other more distant relatives.

There are many reasons people must give up their gallbladders, but the chief reason they lose them is that they have been eating too much fat, and often that fat is part of what is supposed to be an accessory dish that being able to prepare perfectly was once a measure of feminine accomplishment. That dish is called "gravy." If your gravy was smooth and tasty, you had the sensibilities of a real lady. If your gravy was lumpy, well, my dear, if you slept on a mattress that had a pea under it, you wouldn't feel a thing and you certainly weren't a Southern Princess named Belle.

Making gravy, like drawing and playing the piano, was one of the measures of feminine accomplishments back before people knew it wasn't good for your digestion. As a consequence of that philosophy, previous generations of women worked hard at perfecting their gravies. I still have my gallbladder, and I credit this retention to the fact that I both resist making gravy and I resist eating gravy.

However, I believe in knowing how to make gravy when I want to show off. So, here's how your grandmother Lola and your Aunt Mary Ellen taught me how to make Southern woman gravy. Each one was a superior, refined lady, and each one had a different approach to making gravy. Let that be the lesson—not the recipe for the gravy itself!

Lola's Southern Woman Gravy

What you need:

Flour (about ½ cup)

Drippings

A diced onion

A big pan

Some warm water in a nearby glass

A slotted spoon for stirring

Salt and pepper

How your grandmother made the gravy:

Your grandmother made gravy from heavy drippings. This name is what you call the condensed fat in a pan after you have cooked a big piece of meat like a roast. Your mother liked onions in her gravy and diced them and browned them in the pan with the drippings. Then, she spooned in a couple of big tablespoons of flour and browned that.

Next, with an extra pair of hands of any of her daughters at the ready to take over the urgent stirring of the flour, Mother began to drizzle warm water into the pan, stirring intently until a brown paste emerged. Salt and pepper were added then. More water followed. "More water!" More stirring. "More water! Get that lump! Strain that lump!" Gravy should be served hot and not lumpy.

Mom did this until about half the pan was full of water and the liquid reached a simmering state. It was a big pot of gravy. She was cooking for a large crowd. "Keep stirring," she urged. Arms and hands grew tired with this stirring. It was more taxing than beating hot fudge to cool it.

Throughout the adding of water, Mother tasted what is supposed to be an accessory dish and which required the effort of the entree itself until she had enough gravy to return the meat to it if she was making country fried steak. If she was making a roast, the meat stayed on the plate and the gravy was served on top of creamed potatoes (made with two sticks of butter and whole milk).

As you can see, gravy partnered with beef, often, and vegetables that had been cooked in butter. Because its base is condensed-fat, it is a fat-full meal. Gallbladders can't take the overload and eventually rebel.

That said, gravy is very tasty and while served as a complement to meats in our generation, previously gravy had a real job to do and that was to be poured over bread, biscuits, and rice to stretch a meal that was short on meat or the next meal that was a left-over and had no meat at all.

You can make some kind of gravy from just about any kind of drippings. Ask your Aunt Julie about Red Eye Gravy if you don't believe me. Ask your cousin Kevin who told me recently, "I can make gravy out of anything."

Here are some ways to make gravy, but your cousin Kevin is right: you can truly invent your own.

Aunt Mary Ellen's Gravy

What you need:

Drippings in a pan

Flour (about ½ cup)

Water—as much as the amount of gravy that you need to cover the meat that you want to simmer in the gravy

Salt and pepper

Directions:

Your aunt Mary Ellen made gravy our mother's way until she figured out her own way to do it, and that was to spoon flour into a very tall glass, add salt and pepper, then hot water. When Mary Ellen showed me how to do it, she stirred this mixture in the glass vigorously with a fork. Then she added the flour/water mixture to her drippings. The end result? Less stirring and fewer lumps. This procedure was hard for your grandmother to accept, and your Aunt Mary Ellen, who is known for being a hard worker, had a hard time working less hard even though she is the one who discovered this method and taught it to me. You either serve this gravy on the side or make enough to smother the meat you are cooking in it, and let that meat simmer until it can be cut with a fork. In the North, people call that kind of meat over-cooked. In the South, we call that kind of meat, tender. To get very colloquial, it is sometimes referred to as "gum-smacking good." (Gum-smacking means that even toothless people can chew meat this tender.)

Mary Ellen's gravy is thinner than your grandmother's and very tasty. She doesn't use onions.

I don't either.

Aunt Guin's Cream Gravy

What you need:

Flour (about ½ cup)

Milk

Drippings

Salt and pepper

Guin says:

"I serve this cream gravy over cornbread with fried chicken, but I also make it with salmon croquettes."

Directions:

"Use a clean skillet—not the one you fried the chicken in (or the salmon croquettes). In that clean skillet, you ladle about four tablespoons of the grease you used to fry chicken (more if you need more gravy), and add flour to create a paste. Add salt and pepper and then slowly drizzle in the milk. You will need to keep the temperature on low and continue stirring until the flour thickens with the milk. When it does, it happens fast. Remove it from heat. Serve over cornbread when you make fried chicken. Serve it over the salmon croquettes if that's what you make."

Your Grandmother's Country Fried Steak

What you need:

Round steak or ground meat to make patties

A drizzle of oil in the skillet

Flour (about ½ cup or more)

Salt and pepper

Directions:

Brown your meat on both sides in a skillet. Then, add the flour/water mixture your Aunt Mary Ellen devised. Stir a couple of minutes. It will be lumpy. Add more water. Return the meat. The lumps cook themselves out if you just keep adding water.

Beloved,

I don't make gravy much anymore, but I could if someone in the family was coming over and requested your grandmother's signature dish of country fried steak and creamed potatoes. Visiting relatives still want that meal from time to time when they come to visit. Family reunions are fewer than ever these days except for funerals and weddings, and I rarely make country fried steak unless I am feeling homesick for mother. When I make it, I don't eat very much, but I do feel it is a kind of visit with my mother, and it tastes very good. Just remember, that fats taste great, but they are not always your friend. However, flour always is.

Flour, like eggs, often holds ingredients together. Flour mixes have gained popularity in our country since long before Betty Crocker's Bisquick. Before Betty there was a controversial character played by an actress and named Aunt Jemima, who became famous at the 1893 World's Fair in Chicago where the pancake mix bearing her name was introduced to the people who came to the Fair.

At the Fair, Aunt Jemima was called the Pancake Queen, because she made pancakes, and while she was cooking she told stories about how the mix came into being. Talking while you cook is one of the ways that traditions get passed along and family folklore gets born!

Actually the pancake mix was invented by Chris Rutt, who didn't keep control of the product for very long. He chose the name after he heard a song about old Aunt Jemima in a Vaudeville show. That's a type of entertainment you may not know, but there's a resurgence of the type of big gag routines showing up in various entertainment venues that I shall not mention here because I do not want to get into a public argument with strangers. However, the Aunt Jemima character at the World's Fair made pancakes and served them to Fair-goers and told stories of how she once upon a time had worked on a plantation and invented the famous pancake recipe and was now, at the behest of the Old Colonel and out of a spirit of largesse, taking the gift of this pancake recipe to the world.

The Aunt Jemima icon has become seriously controversial over time. The changes in the Aunt Jemima image parallel in some ways the modifications of Betty Crocker's ever-evolving appearance. They both ended up prettified and wearing pearls. When you see the series of photographs of the images of each woman in chronological order, you will note that their outfits have been changed to reflect the times of fashion and the way society has seen women as belonging mostly in the kitchen—only these two women both came out of the kitchen and still cooked when they wanted to and the ways they wanted to. The hair styles have been updated. The kerchief was taken off of Aunt Jemima's head, and later on, Betty Crocker's image was created with a darkened skin tone to represent more of the non-white population. Those series of pictures of each woman remind me of the grade school pictures that many people take of children and on into adulthood to create a kind of pictorial timeline of growth. Whether it's the pictures of two companies' icons or the images of a child growing up, neither the series nor any individual photos strung together or hung together on a wall tell the story of a human being's life or even a business icon's influence on shaping a company's image. Think about that string of images sometimes, Beloved, and know this: the stories of our lives get told in a kind of linear way with photos and anecdotes and memories pointing to places of change that are commemorated, like your wedding photos will one day.

But a bride lives longer than that, and she never stops being a bride. As old as you may become all of the times of your life stay inside of you, and you continue to always be a child, a girl, a young lady, a bride, and then someone whom others call older, which is a funny word. People use that word to mean that you have reached an age when you are no longer considered young with a bright and uncharted future ahead of you. But that's not what it really means. Being older means that you live a fuller life with a great recognition that time and the experience of time is not measured in a linear way—it happens all at once all at the same time and expands and makes being alive bigger and bigger and bigger. Think about taking small breaths. Then take a bigger breath—filling your lungs with the goodness of life. Being older means that. Taking bigger and bigger breaths of life and expelling pain, fear, doubt, judgment, self-recrimination, and even mournfulness because over time the great sorrows and loss that come to everyone are part of what makes a good day very good indeed.

When your cousin Lola Leigh got married, the wedding happened just after your grandmother's death—the woman for whom she was named. Lola Leigh was very special to your grandmother. The wedding day happened in spite of the loss, just as my mother—her grandmother—would have wanted and expected. What you don't know is that your grandmother and I went shopping for her outfit to wear to her granddaughter's wedding and that she died before she could wear that fancy royal blue suit with glittery buttons. After mama left us, I returned her wedding suit to the store, got the money and spent the two hundred dollars or so on eleven gifts for her granddaughter Lola because we did cancel her bridal shower. Most of the presents Lola received came from her grandmother, though I am not sure I made that clear. I probably didn't because I would not have wanted to tell the story about returning her grandmother's wedding outfit. Here's the poignant part of the story. The blue suit your grandmother had bought to wear to the wedding was very similar to the same blue suit she had worn for years as the wife of a preacher, and we buried her in that sweet, old worn-out preacher's wife suit. Your grandmother was a magnanimous woman who loved the people in your family in the same way her mother did and the same way her youngest sister, Aunt Judy, is famous for loving people, and which is best summed up in the same stance they have all taken right in front of my eyes from your great grandmother Ruby Pearl to your grandmother Lola and your Aunt Judy. They greet you with open arms and when you leave they freely let you go and say, "I love you arms wide open." Your grandmother and your great-grandmother are waiting for you in eternity now, as I stand in their place with my arms wide open for you—receiving you and letting you go at the same time.

Your grandmother loved you like that, and she would have enjoyed seeing you get married; but I can tell you, she's with you—will always be with you—because the kind of love that we have for one another doesn't stop or ever die. It lives on inside each of us in the sorrow and the joys that follow separation, and it lives on inside the very real presence of the Holy Spirit, who bridges the unimaginable gap from here to heaven, and it lives on inside the love of Jesus whose arms are outstretched through all time welcoming everyone to come unto him.

Just as there are many stories associated with Betty Crocker, Aunt Jemima, your grandmother, your cousin, and you, these stories represent only spots of time, but those moments—precious, both fleeting and eternal, live on.

Here's a story about a dish that accompanies going to funerals—a subject that was much discussed long before your grandparents left this earth and moved in with Jesus full-time.

A Taste of Home...

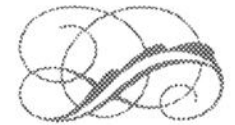

THAT MISSING PIECE OF NORA'S CAKE

Whenever someone dies in our home town, Nora, my parents' friend, takes over one of her famous tube-shaped apricot nectar cakes with a fat piece missing. Nora does what every other cake baker would like to do: she samples her cake before she gives it away. That way she can fall asleep that night knowing that there wasn't some dark, damp uncooked spot in the center which proved either that she was an impatient cook or that her oven had cooked too slowly.

I know this about Nora's apricot nectar cakes although she isn't a friend of mine directly. My mother and dad tell me that Nora does this for every reception that follows the funeral of a friend. She baked one to take to my uncle's funeral last year, but I didn't taste it. My folks say it's fruity, tart though sweet. They should know. The number of funerals that Nora and my parents attend is considerable.

Funerals are a mainstay of social life here in our town and the subject for many a conversation in my parents' home. My sixty-two year old daddy and my fifty-five year old mother are big believers in being prepared for death. They have owned burial plots for years—are two of a very few number of people, I'm sure, who have owned spare burial plots, which they have given away through the years to a couple of needy dead people. Their tombstones have been up long enough to have vines growing over them. The only things missing from the granite slabs are the dates of the deaths. I'm reminded frequently that this pertinent information will have to be added afterwards. I do not like to hear this and try to change the subject. My parents never do. They welcome the opportunity to explore the options inherent in the after-death experience: the funeral.

A couple of months ago, an audacious funeral salesman made the mistake of going by my parents' home on a sales call. My folks invited the funeral salesman to come on inside.

Comfortably situated on the sofa, they interviewed the funeral salesman aggressively, compared what they had already reserved for themselves to the package he was selling, received willingly his brochures, and sent him on his way. Then, because they are thorough investigators, they paid a surprise call on him at his business establishment–the funeral home. They were shocked at the high price of his poorly constructed caskets and full of self-congratulations that they had foreseen the terrible inflation of funeral costs long ago and bought the only real insurance—a prepaid funeral. They left certain in their souls that the funeral salesman's proposal was, if not crooked, certainly over-priced.

Through the week, they warned all their friends about that guy in the dark blue suit going from door to door in this small town attempting to prey on people who would eventually die. They warned me. No one is going to come to our town and get away with selling an over-priced funeral. There are just too many comparison shoppers here, although my parents, the youngest of their crowd, are the acknowledged experts on funeral preparedness.

"You wanna go out and see where our plots are again?" my father inquired once more.

"Nope. Sure don't."

"The time's gonna come and you're not gonna remember where to plant us."

I laughed. "I don't know why you're going to so much trouble. I'm just going to plant you out in the back yard so I won't have to drive into town to put fresh plastic flowers on your graves. I'm thinking I'll put you right out back underneath the magnolia tree. There's plenty of room for both you and mama. I may not even have to buy flowers. Those magnolias will bloom and get ripe and fall right on top of your graves. I tell you what: I'll even turn up the TV at five o'clock so Mother can still listen to Jeopardy."

What could be more natural?

Sometimes when my father initiates this familiar dialogue, I change the plan and say, "I'm gonna stick you out there alongside Still Creek so you can keep those beavers that you like so well company."

My father hates it when I describe my alternative scheme, though he plays along. "Now, don't go be doing that. We'll be washing up every time those beavers rebuild that blasted dam and the rains come in too heavy."

We laugh again, and Mom and Dad file away the details of our conversation so they can tell them to Nora, who will enjoy the story. They fret though that I haven't actually heard any of the real plans they've been making.

I have. Dad insists that when his time comes a recording of Jeannette McDonald and Nelson Eddy singing "Sweet Mystery of Life" be played. He's not joking. He loves that song.

And I do know right where those grave plots are, and I recall that we will have to order the grave opened, but we must not let them do that on a Sunday because grave diggers get time and a half that day. I do know they've saved an extra grave plot for me; and when they remind me, I take the cue and assure them brightly, "I feel just fine. Couldn't feel better." They like to hear the report of my good health. None of their friends will ever admit to feeling well, and when I do, they have good news to pass on to their friend Nora.

"Our baby's just fine, Nora. She's doing just fine. She says she's gonna put us out by the creek when our time comes."

This very morning, Nora and Mom and Dad attended two funerals. They went over to the funeral home at ten to pay their respects to a departed church friend and discovered that their insurance agent had also died and was going to be buried an hour later. They just stayed on for that one.

Usually, while they are away at one of their gatherings, I read the obituary of the newly-deceased, and today I saw that the father of one of my high school friends had also died. I recognized all of the names of the survivors and wondered if Luanne had to help choose the coffin and buy the concrete vault. Did Luanne know about the grave diggers?

Suddenly, I hoped her mama had a friend who would take over a warm cake with a piece missing: a hole she wouldn't try to disguise by pushing the ends together. I wanted all grieving people to have friends like Nora who represent that sweet mystery of living called loving your neighbor as yourself.

It seems more and more fitting to me to think of that missing piece of Nora's cake as an undisguisable void in a circle of friends and relatives who faithfully move from house to house in a time of mourning, remembering who their friend was, what he did on his off days, what she liked to cook and wear, and how she couldn't resist putting on fresh eyeliner while the collection was being taken up in church. "I'll recall how everyone who partook of that apricot nectar cake time after time was participating in a silent communion, as if with every sweet tart bite they could rob death of some of its sting.

When Nora's gone, I'll remember her cakes and her husband who demanded his share of a warm piece first as his price for having to live with the tempting smell of it baking.

When my parents are gone, we'll have the stories of their love to tell, of their funeral preparations to recount amongst ourselves, recalling with affection how once they bested the final enemy, not death, but that overpriced funeral salesman.

I shall remember glumly reading the announcement that Luanne's daddy had died, ignoring the part that said he was sixty-two, the same age as my own dad.

When my father came home from that double funeral, I told him about Luanne's dad and about how Luanne and I were best friends in eighth grade. Dad remarked, "I hope that man had a concrete vault already bought. You know the price of concrete has gone sky high."

"I doubt if Luanne gives a damn about the price of concrete," I said.

My father cannot imagine anyone not caring about the price of concrete.

My mother stole a minute away from watching Jeopardy to tell me not to say "damn" out loud in her house, and then she settled back for Double Jeopardy, a sturdy woman unafraid of death. She is at peace about how her daughters will live with grief. She and Dad have done everything they know to teach us how to accept the unacceptable.

They have already paid the bills.

They have set good examples of being faithful friends to their friends.

They have shown us how to mourn—by remembering the good in each other, making light of the bad, and by laughing at the absurdities of human nature. All we girls have left to do is order the dates inscribed on those tombstones already standing on the grave plots they have owned for years. Then, I imagine we'll listen to Nelson Eddy and Jeannette McDonald sing "Sweet Mystery of Life" one more time.

What could be more natural?

Apricot Nectar Cake

A Lemon box cake (Betty Crocker)

A can of apricot nectar (they sell these in the fruit juice aisle)

A cup or so of Confectioner's sugar—more if you like a lot of glaze (I don't really measure)

Butter—about a half stick

Milk—about a quarter of a cup

Directions:

A Bundt pan (which is different from a tube pan and sometimes you will hear a tube pan called a stem pan because it has that single pole "stem" coming up through the base)

Make the Lemon cake substituting apricot nectar for the liquid. Reserve some for the glaze, but it doesn't take much liquid to make a glaze and you can always add a little lemon juice if you don't have enough nectar. If you don't have a lemon and there isn't enough nectar left in the can, add the water to reach the amount that you need. Bake the cake in a Bundt pan.

Glaze

What you need:

Confectioner's sugar

Vanilla extract

Some apricot nectar and maybe some lemon juice if you don't have enough nectar

Some butter if you decide you want a thicker glaze—two-three tablespoons of butter, softened

Directions:

Just stir the sugar and the nectar and a splash of vanilla extract together until you achieve a very thin consistency. Then, pour this over the cake. If you want a thicker glaze, start with about 2-3 tablespoons of softened butter and blend. Adding the butter makes a thicker glaze, but I like this glaze very thin—the same thinness of a glazed doughnut. (Less butter means a thinner glaze.)

When the cake is cool, drizzle on the glaze.

Take it to a grieving family. It will help them.

By the way, **The Atlanta Constitution** bought this essay, and my editor said that his boss came down when he read it and said, "This is the kind of writing we always want in this newspaper." I thought then: 'My publishing life is secured.' I was wrong. That was the death of me at that newspaper.

Section 6
Comfort Foods

What's in this section:

Scrambled eggs

Chicken Noodle Soup

Chicken Pot Pie

Chicken Salad

Bride's Delight

Homemade Cocoa

A Taste of Home: *Fever Pitch*

Beloved,

When you are sick or your husband is ailing, you will need to be able to cook or have dishes that help you to feel better. These are the dishes people call comfort foods traditionally. You like comforting creamed potatoes when you are ailing. And, you like scrambled egg whites, too. I do not know what your husband-to-be will want when he doesn't feel well—or when he's homesick, but an ailment can represent an aspect of homesickness. Chances are, you will feel homesick for a while, and you will move around a great deal as a military wife. You will learn the rhythm of that and how to pack and unpack and what to cook when your kitchen isn't fully set up—and when it is. Your list of comfort foods will grow as you grow older together in your marriage. But you will most likely always come back to the scrambled eggs and the creamed potatoes (Just boil the peeled potatoes until tender, drain the water well, add butter, salt, pepper and milk. A little milk goes a long ways so start small. If you want them real creamy, use a mixer. If you don't mind a few lumps, use that hand-held potato masher. It's quicker and washes easily in the dishwasher.)

You may think that scrambling an egg is simple, but really good scrambled eggs require care. Some days you won't care. Other days you will. There are varying degrees of really good scrambled eggs, and I never scramble eggs that I don't think of a woman named Celaine who scrambled eggs for me when she was a maid in our house for a brief while.

She made the best scrambled eggs I have ever tasted, but she left us before I learned why they were the best. This is often a pattern in my life—to taste something and be unable to find out why it was so good. But scrambled eggs! I eat them often, and the best ones in my memory—and at eyesight level (I was a kid at the time) – were mysteriously browned in the skillet, and for a long time I thought Celaine scorched the butter in the skillet and then added the beaten eggs, but now I think she used a teaspoon of bacon grease instead of butter to coat the small skillet and then added the beaten eggs. I think she also cooked them in an iron skillet, because when I was a kid, coated pans had not been invented and iron skillets were universally used for cooking all kinds of dishes.

A great-grandmother you never met used an iron skillet to make her banana bread, and it was crusty the way cornbread is. I liked that banana bread, but I don't use an iron skillet for mine. I use a loaf pan that I coat with butter—not a cooking spray like Pam. There are many dishes for which I prefer the taste of butter and banana bread and scrambled eggs are two; but some day before I die, I may use a teaspoon of bacon grease in an iron skillet to make scrambled eggs, although I fear going down that slippery slope since bacon grease isn't good for you. And it is not convenient because we don't keep bacon grease stored in jars in the refrigerator much anymore because we microwave our bacon, mostly to drain off the grease on a paper towel. We used to collect and store bacon grease in small jars to season our beans when we cooked them. Sometimes I still do when I know I will be making beans soon.

But in my growing-up years, bacon grease in a jar was always in the refrigerator, and I suspect that Celaine used it for her eggs but I do not and I do use butter sometimes or, more often, that cooking spray Pam if I don't care whether my eggs taste particularly good or not.

That will come to you in time—do you just need eggs or do you want to eat truly delicious scrambled eggs?

If it is the latter, here's how you make them. Now, are you wondering why I didn't place this recipe in the section on eggs? Logically I should have. But, I had a judgment call to make—did scrambled eggs belong in a section called eggs or one called comfort foods? You can deduce something about me by drawing your own conclusion, and I shall leave that to you.

Delicious Scrambled Eggs

What you need:

Eggs

A skillet

Real butter—the more the better

A dollop of milk—Half & Half if you have it in the house or even evaporated milk

Salt and pepper

Directions:

Get your skillet hot. Melt the butter but don't let it scorch.

Beat your eggs vigorously with a good fork. Once they are in the skillet, use a big spoon to fold them gently over and over—this is my definition of scrambling. Turn the heat down immediately so that they cook slowly—it's just a couple of minutes tops, but if you cook them slowly they will be tender and not dry.

Do not scrape the stuff off the sides of the skillet. It's stringy and unappetizing. Just serve the eggs themselves.

Lightly buttered toast is better than heavily buttered toast, and if nausea is the problem don't use butter on the toast. Serve the toast dry.

Scrambled eggs are a universal food if you are not feeling well.

So is Chicken Noodle soup, but if you are ill, you won't feel like making it. I make Chicken Noodle soup when I feel well and freeze the extra soup in quart containers for when I don't feel like cooking and when I don't feel well. It freezes nicely and comes in very handy also when a friend becomes ill and you need to take something to someone. Do that whenever you can. Healthy people should attend to ailing ones, always. It is our responsibility and a pleasure.

Chicken Noodle Soup:

Ingredients I use:

Chicken—boiled or left-over chicken from baked chicken

Chicken broth—store-bought or from some you may have stored in your freezer

Onion

Celery

Carrots

Noodles of any size

Salt and pepper

Optional:

Fresh mushrooms

Diced bell pepper for color and crunch

Directions:

Boil a couple of chicken breasts with the skin on in water that covers the chicken—watch it closely and add water if it cooks down. I place a couple of stalks of celery in the broth to add flavor. When the chicken first begins to boil, impurities float to the top. Scoop that off and throw it out so that it doesn't stay in your broth. You may have to add more water more than once.

When meat is fork-cutting tender (about an hour and a half)—lift the chicken out of broth and place it onto a plate where the meat can cool until you can touch it.

Start with a fresh big pot and scoop the broth into it, leaving behind the pan you boiled it in because there's a ring around the inside that strikes me as unsavory.

Beginning with your fresh broth, add thinly diced celery, thinly sliced carrots, and egg noodles.

Salt, pepper, and if you like a stronger chicken taste add more broth or condensed chicken base you can find in the stores now. Simmer until veggies are tender.

Serve hot with cornbread or Saltines.

On days when the whole cut-up fryers are on sale, I buy the whole fryer instead and boil it all. There is a great deal of meat. I divide the cooked meat and make a chicken pot pie and chicken salad. The chicken pot pie is a good idea because it uses many of the same ingredients as the soup but differently.

Chicken Pot Pie

Here's what you need:

Some chicken meat (the meat from a couple of chicken breasts or a mixed amount of white and dark pieces if you have boiled or baked a whole chicken)

Two prepared pie crusts

A medium-sized Pyrex deep-dish pie plate or casserole dish

Pam spray

A handful of frozen peas (You don't need many, and they are more for color and decoration than food.)

Pre-cooked slices of carrot—Boil them for a couple of minutes to get them tender.

Directions:

Spray the Pyrex dish.

Take one of the pie crusts and gently tear it into about one inch wide strips. (Can be wider if you like) Layer the strips on the bottom of the dish the way you might lasagna.

Add a handful of chicken and add peas and carrots.

Layer another line of pie crust strips.

Add chicken, peas, and carrots. (You can add pearly onions or those small baby ears of corn.)

Cover all ingredients with broth—about two cups. You want the broth to cover the ingredients but not drown the top crust that you place on top. You can layer strips again or use the whole other pie crust for this. I use the whole crust because I like a lot of crust and I have never been very adept at braiding strips of crust though that looks very pretty.

Then, if you have used the whole crust, pierce the top with a fork, making about five x's. The broth will seep up through the holes. Don't worry about that. It will be good.

Bake until golden brown, about 45-50 minutes at 350 degrees. Feeds three hungry people or two with leftovers, but chicken pot pie served as leftovers is not very appetizing.

Chicken Salad

What you need:

Cooked chicken leftover or cooked just to make the salad—it can be baked or boiled (but not canned)

Mayonnaise

Salt and pepper

Celery salt

Chopped celery

Optional ingredients:

Chopped nuts—walnuts or pecan

Dried cranberries, dried cherries, dried blueberries—it's all good.

Grapes, although I like these more served on the side

Toasted almonds

Kevin's tip: "Make sure you drain your pickle relish with a fork so that you don't add too much liquid."

Directions:

Just chop the meat and the celery and mix both with mayonnaise. Salt and pepper. Add any dried fruit you like.

Less mayonnaise is best so start with a little and add till you have the texture you want.

Salt, pepper, and add celery salt.

I serve this with crackers or warm rolls (I keep Sister Schubert's Parker House rolls in the freezer and they are perfect with chicken salad.)

Bride's Delight

You didn't like this Jell-O salad dish growing up, but most other people do. I made it for you recently, and you said, "It's not entirely horrible."

You were being polite.

You don't like Bride's Delight because it has Cool Whip in it, and the texture doesn't suit you. However, your grandmother always made this side dish—usually at Easter because the color looks good with ham, which is the entrée for Easter—so I am including this recipe in case you ever change your mind. Is it a comfort food? Not if you find it horrible, but not everyone does—and for some people, when they miss their mother during the holidays, it is a comfort food.

You will need:

One large box of Lime Jell-O

A cold Sprite or ginger ale

Small container of Cool Whip

Small container of cottage cheese

Small can of chilled crushed pineapple, which you drain before you add to the salad

Pecans (chopped), if you like

Cherries, if you make it at Christmastime and want to go red and green.

Directions:

Prepare the Jell-O. Use the hot water as directed, but instead of adding the cold water called for on the box to fill out the recipe, add chilled Sprite instead.

Place the bowl in refrigerator until it is semi-set. Then, stir in the other ingredients. Put it back in the refrigerator to finish setting. Serve as a side dish at dinner or as dessert.

Homemade Cocoa

What you need:

A cold and sleepless night

A window with a view of a full moon

Milk

Cocoa

Sugar

Hot water

A heavy-bottomed saucepan

So many people have machines that make cocoa now or buy mixes for cocoa that they do not know that the very best cup of cocoa you can make comes directly from the can marked Cocoa.

If you are feeling poorly or suffer from insomnia, a cup of cocoa made from scratch tastes better than an instant cup from a mix or from a machine.

Directions:

Heat the milk slowly on the stove.

While it is heating, put about a teaspoon of cocoa in your cup and about three teaspoons of sugar. Use just enough hot water to melt and combine the cocoa and the sugar. Stir thoroughly.

Add the hot milk and stir.

When made this way, you do not need marshmallows or whipped cream on top because it is plenty rich enough just the way it is.

Beloved,

Men and women respond to being sick differently and they have different views about what to eat and how to be a caregiver. Here's a story to help you understand some of those differences.

The Sounds of Home....

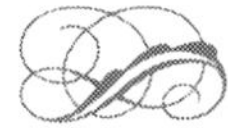

FEVER PITCH

"He was sick all last week, and you know what that's like. He said he didn't have an appetite, which is just his way of saying that he won't eat anything normal. You know what that means?"

I grunted ambiguously into the telephone. It was a sufficient response to keep my friend talking about her ailing husband.

"Well, three meals a day, every day he was sick, I had to think of something special to fix for him to eat. And, of course, he couldn't come to the table to eat it. Wherever he was sitting, I had to take his food to him and stand next to him while he ate the first bite because it might be too hot for him, and he didn't have the breath, he said, to blow on his own food. So I blew on it for him, and told him, "Don't burn your tongue, now darlin'.'

"Do you know how hard that is–to blow on someone else's food without spitting?

I won't be winning any assertiveness training awards from Gloria Steinem, but then, that woman's not practiced at being married, so she doesn't really know what it's like here in the trenches.

"It's okay to fight for equal rights when your man is well enough to stand being told he's wrong, but a woman can't argue with a man when he's sick because he's likely to curl up in a ball and die on her, and then she's stuck with the memory that she killed him."

Before I could verify that my friend really thought her husband might kick the bucket if she told him he was wrong, she offered another revelation.

"I can't tell you how many times I've imagined myself standing next to my husband's grave as we lowered his casket into the ground, and I'm thinking, `This is my fault. If I could just have told him he was right one more time while he was sick, he might still be alive today.' Anyway, when he's ailing, I cook myself crazy trying to please him."

I thought that was an accurate diagnosis because she sounded crazy to me.

"Of course, it's a whole different ball game when a woman gets sick," she declared. "He'll contradict you night and day because he thinks he knows what's good for you. I learned early on that when I'm sick, I might as well resign myself to dying or living on Saltine crackers because if I'm depending on my husband for food, I might as well join the birds outside and start hunting for worms.

"The last time I had a cold all I asked of my Sweet Thang was that he go to the store and buy me a can of chicken noodle soup. I begged him to buy me a simple can of chicken noodle soup, because that's all I thought I could swallow.

"Do you know what he came back with? He brought back a can of that chunky beef stew with lardlike potatoes. He told me that the beef would be better for me than the chicken, and when I told him that I did not think I could swallow hunks of grease, he actually told me I was being a difficult patient.

"To make up with him I had to tell him he was right one more time by eating every drop of that soup that he kept explaining he had made a special trip to the grocery store to buy. And you bet your life I couldn't stay sick for long. When he said he was going to go and buy me a case of that beef stew to last the week, I got myself out of the bed and told him I was all right, which I guess, means that in his own way, he did help me get well.

"He called me a few minutes ago. This was his first whole day back to work after being sick, and he said he was coming home for lunch and asked what I was making. I couldn't believe my ears. I don't cook a hot lunch except when he's here, and you'd think after all these years he would know that. I didn't tell him that though, because the news might have put him into a relapse, and I don't think I could live through that. I tried to break it to him easy. I said, 'Don't you and the boys eat barbecue at The Smokehouse on Mondays?'"

"He said in that low pitiful voice men get sometimes, `I want to come home.' You know how a man can say those words?"

"No, I don't," I replied truthfully. "I'm not married, remember?"

"I am," she replied thoughtfully. "And I love Sweet Thang to death and I'm glad he's well again, but when he gets here, I may have to shoot him."

This article appeared originally in **The Chicago Tribune.**

Section 7

What to take to a Potluck or Fellowship Supper

What's in this section....

Chicken Poppy Seed Casserole

Aunt Daphne's Fried Chicken

Aunt Judy's I-Love-You-Arms-Wide-Open Lasagna

Cherry Cobbler

Strawberry Pie

Baked Ham

A Taste of Home: *Church Lady Chicken Supreme*

Beloved.....

From time to time, you will find yourself in a social situation where you and someone else have brought the same dish to a covered-dish affair where the guests pitch in to provide the food.

The chicken dish that most often shows up at these large gatherings has a variety of names but for the purpose of explaining the tricky dynamic of taking a dish to a covered-dish event, we'll call this dish:

Chicken Poppy Seed Casserole

Right away, if you are of a certain age, you wonder about the insidious effects of poppy seeds catching in your front teeth or getting in between bridge work, and people with diverticulitis have a hard time digesting small seeds of any kind (blackberries, strawberries). So, when you are planning which dish to take, keep in mind that older people have dental issues and often diverticulitis (avoid seeds), so plan accordingly.

That said, even though I am lactose intolerant and have a very real trepidation about ingesting seeds, I made a Chicken Poppy Seed Casserole to take to a social gathering because I had most of the ingredients on hand and did not want to go to the grocery store.

The ingredients I used:

Ritz crackers

Two cans of white-meat chicken

Two cans of Cream of Chicken soup

A tub of sour cream

A teaspoon of poppy seeds

Some butter (as much or as little as you like—I consider a half stick enough, melted)

A disposable 9 inch by 13 inch tin foil pan, because I do not like to try and wash a dish at someone's house to get it home, and I don't want to leave a dish that makes someone else responsible for returning it to me (You will see a number of these casserole dishes at gatherings with names labeled in Sharpie on the side on a piece of masking tape, but do not copy that move. Just buy disposable pans and use them. In life you will have many opportunities to look pretty or be smart. Pick smart.)

How I made the casserole:

So, I mixed up my casserole by combining the chicken with the soup, stirring in a spoonful of poppy seeds and layering the pan with the mixture. Then, I added crunched-up Ritz crackers for a top crust. Some people add grated cheese into the crushed crackers for flavor. I didn't have any. I baked the whole shebang just before it was to be delivered. Then I wrapped an old cloth around it that I wouldn't mind losing and took it to the party. The church kitchen is full of these towels, odd spoons and coffee mugs that people who work at the church a lot take there and leave so that they can drink coffee in a kind of cup they like. Beware when you see cups like that in the church kitchen. Do not use them any more than you would sit on someone else's pew.

There are many rules like this for how to navigate church life successfully, and they are not written down in the Bible. But here are my top 10:

1. When possible volunteer to take rolls, potato chips or gallons of tea. There can be an unspoken competition among church

women to bring the best or most popular dish. Stay out of it. No one competes with a jug of sweet tea.

2. In the kitchen during clean up, pretend you don't hear the endless jokes about Martha in the kitchen while Mary is out in the dining hall fellowshipping. There is a kind of veiled aggression in these jokes that it is best to ignore.

3. When it's time to leave the event, simply excuse yourself to go to the restroom and slip out the side door and go home, unless you are good at the kind of farewell small talk that many people can make comfortably. I can't and don't so I leave like this.

4. If you decided that you cannot stand how messy or greasy the stove looks at church, do not clean it up during or immediately after the fellowship supper. Again, more jokes will be made about Martha and you. They aren't funny. Just go back up there during the work day and clean the stove. Jesus does not judge you for these impulses. There is nothing wrong with wanting a clean stove.

5. When people want to vote about whether to serve only caffeinated coffee or decaffeinated coffee at Fellowship Suppers, abstain from voting. That is one of the most cantankerous discussions that can ensue—right up there with full immersion baptism versus sprinkling.

6. Never under any circumstances suggest to the preacher that Murphy's Oil Soap wipes be put out on the end of pews so that when folks are kneeling in prayer they can spot clean those dusty places on the floor between the pews which the clean-up crew is missing.

7. When you take fudge to any Christmas gathering be prepared to have late-night phone calls from new admirers wanting a second

helping. Go ahead and make another batch. This is truly an act of mercy if you have perfected my fudge recipe.

8. When asked to bring a cake, do not take a chocolate cake. Take that Butter Pecan cake instead. People are used to eating chocolate cake but that Butter Pecan cake is a stand-out. You are not competing with this cake. You are showing them a different kind of cake, which results in flexible thinking—and that is a strongly desired and oft-needed turn of mind in congregations that lean toward Puritanism.

9. Be careful about collecting recipes from people who lived through the Depression. I have a recipe for fried chicken that calls for cooking oil to which you add bacon grease and then a stick of butter. Indeed, it makes very tasty chicken, but that's three types of fat. You don't need all that fat. The three-fats recipe derives from needing to pool the kinds of fat that were available in the Depression-time home in order to have enough cooking oil to fry chicken. If you ever read a recipe that calls for an over-abundance of ingredients like this, consider the heritage of that recipe and make adjustments. It was most likely invented during the Depression, and you can safely make exchanges in the ingredients that are healthier choices.

10. If an extra serving spoon is reported as having been left behind in another church lady's home where she hosted the Sunday school class' annual Christmas get-together, do not say it is yours even if it is yours. Just let it go. See my story about the spinach dip bowl if you need a reminder about how things can disappear, get claimed and still be considered stolen. In short, never place yourself in the position of being accused of having stolen another woman's serving spoon. Better to let the spoon go then have that accusation hanging over your head.

Beloved,

Do you want my recipe for fried chicken without butter and bacon grease?

Here it is.

Aunt Daphne's Fried Chicken

The ingredients:

A cut-up chicken, washed thoroughly, skinned or not

Enough oil to fill the frying pan to about halfway

Enough whole buttermilk to marinade the chicken in

A small bag of self-rising flour and a big Ziploc bag to hold and shake the chicken

Salt and pepper

Directions:

Wash the cut-up chicken thoroughly and wash your hands and the faucet handle in the kitchen because you cannot keep your kitchen too clean.

Then, put that chicken in a big bowl and cover it with buttermilk. Cover the bowl. Put it back in the fridge for about two hours. (It can be less than that, but two hours tenderizes it.)

Get a gallon-size Ziploc bag and dump in a small bag of self-rising flour.

Add some salt and pepper.

Put your skillet on the stove and fill it to about midway with your cooking oil.

Set the heat for 4 or so and then be ready to raise the temperature.

Take your chicken out of the fridge and place it piece by piece on a big plate that can drain off the excess buttermilk. Add more salt and pepper.

Place the milk-soaked pieces in the Ziploc bag, zip it closed (double check that because it makes a mess if you're wrong), and shake the bag of chicken to coat it completely in flour.

Check your oil to see if it is hot enough. Flick a drop of water into the skillet. If it hisses back at you it's ready.

Lay one piece of chicken in the oil. You're probably up to 5-6 on the temperature dial now.

Leave a little room between the pieces of chicken so that the oil can reach up around the sides of each piece.

Monitor the heat because when you place more chilled chicken in the skillet the heat reduces.

Try to keep the heat even.

Watch it. The chicken will start browning up the sides. When that happens, turn the chicken over, being careful not to slosh the grease over the sides of the skillet.

Have a big plate with a paper towel on it ready to receive the fried chicken.

If you are cooking a lot of chicken you will need two plates. Don't drain one piece of chicken on top of another piece of chicken. Drain each piece individually.

Turn off the skillet and set it aside to cool. Do not fool with that hot grease while it is hot. Let the pan cool for as long as you can stand the mess sitting on the stove.

Then, pour the grease into a big jar with a lid that you can tighten. Let the liquid cool some more if you need to before you throw it away. Some people store grease and reuse it. Do that only if you made homemade French fries and plan to make them again very soon. Otherwise, throw out the grease. It's not worth the indigestion that follows from reusing grease. When you do try to dispose of the grease, pour it into a big-mouth jar or use a funnel. I can never seem to find my funnel, but I do save mayonnaise jars for this, and they work pretty well.

Do not pour grease down your kitchen sink. If the grease overflows the container, immediately squirt a great deal of grease-fighting detergent, like Dawn, and run very hot water down the drain. I don't know if that helps, but your granddaddy made us do that and we do a lot of stuff around the house that he told us to do. I still believe him about a lot of things.

Chances are you won't take fried chicken to a potluck dinner because it doesn't stretch far enough to be your share. Your Aunt Judy understands that problem, and she says, "Take lasagna." You shouldn't know Aunt Judy only from her postings on Facebook or this recipe. You should know this additional fact about her. She loves you "arms wide open." That's how she greets you in her prayers and in person. It is a way of loving other people that she inherited from her mother, your great-grandmother Ruby Pearl Morris, who always loved everyone arms wide open too. When you take Aunt Judy's lasagna to potluck dinners, people will feel loved like that. Here's her recipe.

Aunt Judy's "I-Love-You-Arms-Wide-Open Lasagna"

What you will need:

Package of lasagna noodles (Boil them and get them ready to use in the pan.)

2 lbs. of ground beef

1 large chopped onion

1 can of tomatoes (I prefer the petite diced)

2 6 oz. cans of tomato paste

1 tablespoon chopped parsley if it is dried

2 tablespoons chopped parsley if it is fresh

2 teaspoons salt

1 teaspoon sugar

1 teaspoon of garlic powder

½ teaspoon of Oregano leaves

16 oz. each of Ricotta or small curd Cottage cheese, Mozzarella, Swiss and grated Parmesan

Directions:

Brown meat. Combine all ingredients. Simmer for 30 minutes. Use at least a 13 x 9 x 2 pan. (I use a bigger one.) Spread some meat sauce on the bottom of the pan to keep it from sticking. Alternate layers of sauce, noodles, cheese. Top with mozzarella. Bake 40-50 minutes. Let stand 15 minutes.

Note from your Aunt Judy: "I like to mix all the cheeses together, except Ricotta. I spread this first. You will need six lasagna noodles. This makes a double layer. I hope you enjoy this. It will feed about eight people."

CHERRY COBBLER

Ingredients:

As many cans of cherry pie filling as you want to use (three-four?—it depends on the size of the crowd and how big a pan you use)

Pie shell– big enough to cover the largest Pyrex dish you have and plan to use

Butter

Sugar

I have had more requests for this dish than any I have made, but even though it is easy to make, I wearied of taking it to church functions, so I stopped a long time ago. It was the lie of it that made me tired. People thought I was really cooking up a storm with this dish, and mainly it was just opening some cans and adding sugar and butter. I got tired of all that admiration for very little work or creative ability. It's not good for your soul to be praised that much for so little effort, but here's the recipe in case you are short on time and want to please people who will really love this dish.

Directions:

In the biggest Pyrex dish you have, pour three or four cans of cherry pie filling. Upon that I sprinkled a half cup of sugar and sliced a half stick of butter in thin slices on top. On top of this I laid a pie crust. I made the requisite steam holes on the top with a fork and then sprinkled very lightly more sugar on the top of the crust. Then I simply baked it at 350 degrees. I had to use a Pyrex dish, which contradicts my very strong stance on using disposable tin foil pans when carrying food elsewhere because the cherries are very heavy and the tin foil pan somehow just doesn't suit this cobbler.

Anyway I used to take this cobbler everywhere. The last time I made it was for a Fellowship Supper at my church where at the end of the evening, two deacons and one elder were standing around my dish with spoons scraping out the last bits of cherry filling because all of the rest of the cherries had been scraped clean. Their wives glared at me as if I were up to no good with that cobbler. Maybe that was the real reason I stopped making it. There are times in your life when it is best to make a dish that people like only in moderation. I think cherry cobbler is one of those dishes.

Here is a safer recipe to take. It's popular and does not trigger competition in others.

Strawberry Pie

Ingredients:

1 cup sugar

1 ¼ cups water

2 tablespoons cornstarch

¼ cup strawberry gelatin powder

4 cups fresh strawberries, halved

1 9-inch baked pie crust

sweetened whipped cream

Directions:

Bring sugar, water and cornstarch to a boil over medium heat.

Cook stirring constantly for 1 minute or until thickened.

Stir in strawberry gelatin until dissolved.

Remove from heat; chill 2 hours.

Arrange your washed strawberries in a pastry shell and pour the gelatin mixture over them.

Cover and chill 2-4 hours.

Serve pie with whipped cream if desired.

Baked Ham

What you need:

A ham (preferably a trimmed ham)

Over-sized tin foil to cover it with

A tin foil pan with handles and a reinforced bottom because it's heavy

Whole cloves

Directions:

Like baking a turkey, baking a ham is far simpler to do than people let on. It achieves a reputation for being difficult because it is the centerpiece of the meal. It is incredibly simple to bake a ham. You just need a roasting pan large enough, oversized tin foil to cover it while it bakes, fresh cloves, and the courage not to add all the stuff people recommend to ostensibly enhance it. Really good baked ham doesn't need those kinds of accessories. It just needs a brave woman who can stand her ground and add only the aromatic cloves, and these are more about whetting the appetites of the people who are in the house while it is baking, slowly.

Buy a smaller ham than you think you need. It goes a long way, and while it is tasty, you do tire of it quickly.

Look for a ham that has been well-trimmed so that you are not paying for fat instead of lean meat.

Try different brands until you know the ones in your current neighborhood that are the best.

8-10 lbs. should be plenty for a dinner party with left-overs for the week

Place the ham in a baking pan that has a heavy bottom. If your oven is large enough to accommodate a big reinforced tin foil pan with handles, that's the way to go. The clean-up is easy. But you will need a great deal of tin foil to cover the ham securely all around the sides.

Peel the wrapper from the ham. Note the cooking time suggested. It is usually something like 20 minutes per pound (or half pound—in this moment, I don't remember).

Sprig cloves around the surface. These are hard to press into the thick skin or meat, but they go easily into the fatty places. Some people do place rings of pineapple on the top and put whole cherries in the middle of each pineapple slice, but that's more for looks than taste, and that fruit just gets in the way when it is time to carve the meat.

Cook the meat slowly.

Serve as the entrée for a dinner; or if cooked over night, serve with biscuits (especially good on Christmas morning).

Beloved,

People have different expectations about how to handle themselves with company, at dinner parties, potluck suppers and any other place where people come together to eat. You may be concerning yourself with the dish to make and how to get it there, and then when you get there, something weird can happen. Here's an example of how something besides eating can go on at potluck suppers and other places.

A Taste of Home....

CHURCH LADY CHICKEN SUPREME

When a man who had studied cooking in Switzerland showed up at the same potluck dinner party carrying basically the same type of Chicken Supreme casserole I had also prepared, I gulped.

As Don whisked his dish out of its thermal sleeve, his casserole was placed in the middle of the other foods, a place of honor as the major entree.

No one told him right away that I had also brought Chicken Supreme, only mine didn't have broccoli in it. His did.

Not big chunks of broccoli—the florets. Don's broccoli had been food processed. I could see all the parts of his chicken dish through his Pyrex dish and everything looked balanced, including the delicate cracker crumbs he had sprinkled on top.

"How did you get your cracker crumbs so fine?" I asked humbly.

His casserole was amazingly neat.

He shrugged artlessly, not inclined to answer my questions about his recipe. Good cooks often don't like to answer questions. It's part of their mystique. I imagined there was an extensive code of cooking tips Don had picked up in Switzerland where chocolate is revered the same way we Southerners value grits.

To fill the awkward silence, I explained my technique: "I pour the tubes of Ritz crackers in a Ziploc bag, and beat them with my fist. It's quite a stress reducer," I added honestly.

"I did not use Ritz crackers," he sniffed, as if my cracker lacked social status. "They are so loaded with fat."

He mumbled the name of some cracker I didn't know that he had specially selected for his dish. I didn't know that they made crackers I didn't know.

About that time, the hostess appeared with my casserole, which had needed warming in the oven because I don't have one of those thermal sleeves that fit a Pyrex dish. Besides, I hadn't used a Pyrex dish. If you want to go home before the eating is finished, you have to leave behind the dish and that means the hostess has to wash it and get it back to you. Out of respect for one another, church ladies use disposable tin foil pans to make meal deliveries easy and clean up simple.

We church ladies have a number of cooking techniques that we willingly tell anyone who will listen. It's not exactly testifying, but we do talk about food–how to cook it, how to carry it, and if we bought our ingredients on sale we'll tell you where to go and how much money you will save, God willing.

I had actually considered using a real glass dish because Chicken Supreme is a heavy entrée; and when I saw the hostess burning her hands a little in order to keep my casserole from dripping, I almost regretted the tin pan. She managed, however, and was able to slide my Chicken Supreme casserole onto the table, positioning my concoction like a bridesmaid next to the bride, which was Don's artistically beautiful dish of Chicken Supreme.

In that moment, I was no longer just a guest at a potluck dinner. I was in a spontaneous cook-off contest with someone who outranked me by both education, reputation, and a cookin' attitude from a foreign country. This tension doesn't usually occur in my daily life where church ladies use the same recipe and compare notes about how big or small to make a dish depending on how many people will need to be fed.

There was twice as much casserole as was needed for the crowd, and I was prepared to lose gracefully–that is, to take home my uneaten casserole– but, to my surprise, it wasn't necessary. Soon, complimentary murmurs were heard amongst the diners who compared notes, "I'm going back for more of hers."

Since I had heard that refrain more than once, so did Don.

We met each other in the kitchen, where he stated the conclusion. "Yours is not a fat-free recipe, is it?" he confirmed, crossing his arms. "You used real sour cream, didn't you?" He said, with wonder in his voice.

"Absolutely," I said.

"I didn't. Mine's low-fat."

"I am so sorry," I said, shaking my head in commiseration. Church ladies may cook fat-free at home to save the lives of their loved ones, but in public, it's butter, sour cream, fat and more of it. I felt for him. It could have happened to anyone. "Your casserole is very pretty though, and that cloth cover you brought it in, well, it's a very well-dressed dish."

I did not explain that I had mistakenly bought fat-free Cream of Chicken soup as one of the primary ingredients of my sauce, and upon reading that Healthy Heart message on the can, I added an extra container of sour cream to make up for that goof. I'd also melted some real butter and drizzled it over the Ritz crackers and it had thinned the sour cream. As a result, my casserole was very soupy, which is why I had also brought along some big fat rolls. A big fat roll can sop up melted sour cream.

No one had needed a bread sponge with Don's casserole, which he was able to neatly return to his special carrying cover.

As I was preparing to leave, the hostess asked me if I wanted to take my limp, messy pan home. I looked at the single cup of remaining goopy casserole and the battered Ritz crackers. "If you don't mind, just toss it in the trash."

"I'll be putting that in my refrigerator for lunch tomorrow," she vowed, silently calculating if there was enough to share with her husband. There wasn't.

Another friend asked me if I would make that dish for her son's wedding reception. "Sure," I said.

"There will be about a hundred people," she added, surprised by my willingness to cook for her. We weren't close, but that doesn't matter: if you are in a church, for whatever reason, a seasoned church lady will help out in the kitchen and volunteer her friends to help out too.

"Not a problem. I'll round up some girls, and we'll make the dish for you," I promised.

We would, too. And we would serve it in our silver-plated chafing dishes that sit on top of those little burning candles. It looks pretty like that. (Nobody understands a wedding reception the way church ladies do or knows more surely that you not only need the help of your friends to make a wedding happen, you rely upon the kindness of acquaintances. When a wedding is a-foot, it's all hands on deck!)

Don, a man unschooled in church lady cooking wisdom, listened intently. He didn't understand what was going on at all.

So as we made our good-byes, I whispered a type of tip about cooking that we ladies pass around to each other in our society where good recipes are a gift we freely give one another. "Don, as a general rule, most people don't like broccoli," I explained softly. "No matter how finely you chop it up."

Section 8
The Katie Days and Snacks

What's in this section:

The Bride-To-Be as a Baby

The Bride-to-Be In Her Bath

The Bride-to-Be At Home with Her Aunt

The Bride-to-Be Dreams of Heaven

The Bride-To-Be Goes Shopping

The Bride-To-Be and Figuring Time

The Bride-to-Be Becomes Herself

The Bride-to-Be Goes To College

Beloved....

You have lived away from home long enough now to have forgotten that we drink coffee about three o'clock in the afternoon. When your grandmother was here to make the coffee pot, there were oatmeal cookies–not homemade oatmeal cookies. Sunshine-brand oatmeal cookies were stored in a really old yellow Tupperware bowl. There were butter cookies that were kept for the dogs, too, and if you wanted a dog cookie with your afternoon coffee you could have it, but those dry thin butter cookies made for humans and bought for the dogs tasted pretty much the way I assume true made-for-dog biscuits would taste: dry. Occasionally, I ate a dog cookie or two if we were out of oatmeal cookies, but mainly I ate the oatmeal cookies–three of them with two cups of coffee, black.

Later in her life your grandmother stopped wanting afternoon coffee and became a Coke girl. She tried to coax me into drinking Coke so she could stop making coffee, but I never converted.

Your granddaddy ate bananas quite famously in the afternoons and considered them the perfect food with his cookies.

Everyone else was at work when you were a child, and so it was just the four of us—three of us adults sipping coffee or Coke and you drinking Sprite from a bottle—one I still have in my cabinet. I imagine hanging it from a Christmas tree as an ornament, but I am somewhat embarrassed to have held on to it for this long. I kept one of your early swimsuits for a long time, too. You may not remember that blue and green swimsuit. You were about three when your grandmother died. You and I were with her when she died, and we prayed together. Later I was holding that swimsuit when you asked me where grandmother had gone, and I showed you the bathing suit that you had only recently outgrown and I said: "Your grandmother outgrew her body and has left it behind like you have outgrown this suit. She lives in heaven now."

You nodded as if you understood me. I said the words automatically, as if that is the only explanation possible for why your grandmother left you—and me. It is that sense that something is true that leads me to include this next series of stories—not pictures, really. Snapshots. I call them my Katie Days stories. This is what it was like to love you as a child and watch a Bride-To Be grow up....and some of the snacks we shared.

The Bride-to-Be as a Baby

Every now and then, my father takes off his baseball cap and tosses it at his newest grandchild, Katie. This time, his cap crests Katie's small round head and falls inside her play pen, which sits in the corner of my parents' large living room.

Katie laughs—adores the game. Pa is disconcerted though. He is losing his touch. The cap is meant to find its mark—that is, Katie's head—and stay there.

"I cannot believe you are playing ring-toss using the baby's head as your target," I moan.

Pa is startled at the critical edge to my voice. "It likes it."

"She," I correct him.

Dad leans over the play pen, retrieves the blue cap, nuzzles its neck, and pretends to have trouble standing upright again. While he is bent over at the waist, Katie pulls that lock of thin gray hair that my father combs from the back of his head to the front to cover his bald space, and she yanks it hard. It is a wiry stretch of hair that we have tried curling, spraying, and fussing at to make it behave. But like the man it belongs to, the hair is unmanageable.

As his lock of hair rises slowly, defying gravity, Pa straightens, and Katie cries out. To placate her, Pa bends again, scoops her up first to his waist, next to his shoulder, and then higher and higher he hoists the toddler until she is sitting on his shoulder. Her arms flail; she hangs onto his hair for support. I catch my breath. It is just a question of time before.....

"This kid isn't afraid of anything," Dad assesses proudly.

The kid is his current favorite granddaughter, whom he and my mother babysit five days a week for nine hours each day. "And, she likes people," he says, eyes twinkling. (He knows she's a girl.) "Never meets a stranger."

"Yes, Katie is sociable," I concur.

Dad adds, "The more people looking at her and talking to her, the better she likes it."

Making airplane sounds, my father lowers Katie back to his waist and settles her into the crook of his elbow. "I was thinking we ought to buy some of those store mannequins and sit them around the room so she could have plenty of company."

I check to see if he is joking. He is not.

"Don't you think that she would figure out the difference before too long?" I ask dryly.

Her Pa doesn't hear me. "Only I don't know where to buy mannequins."

He takes Katie to the couch, where she sits on his belly and pulls at his belt buckle.

"Katie," I whisper. I hold out my arms hopefully. I shake a rattle at her. She only has eyes for her Pa.

Dad takes the rattle from me and says, "Look here. This is a new trick I've taught it." He taps the rattle on Katie's forehead to make her eyes blink. He taps and taps—she blinks and blinks.

"Stop that!" I demand.

"Oh, she likes it," he argues equitably, continuing with the trick.

"Well, her mother and mine wouldn't like it."

Dad shrugs and stops. "Those girls don't know how to have a good time," he says to Katie, as if she isn't one of us.

I reach out again, but Katie takes one long look at me—her aunt—and lets her eyes glaze over. As long as her grandfather is near, she isn't going anywhere else. He is her preferred person.

Pa pulls Katie up to his face and croons something like, "Sit, Spot, sit."

"You treat the baby as if she's a dog," I snip.

"I love dogs," he says, missing my point. "Besides, this little thing has driven Spot crazy. He's so jealous of her."

"Your dog, Spot, was crazy before this baby ever got here."

Katie reaches out and grabs Pa's nose. She pulls on it for a while. She reaches for his glasses. She gnaws on a shoulder bone. Dad is perfectly free with himself. Katie can snack on any part of her granddaddy that she likes.

He wrestles with her in a way that reminds me of his lying on the grass outside while three dogs pounce on him. He buries his head against Katie's stomach and growls. She slaps him on the back of his head and pulls on his hair some more. She is the only person in the family that he lets endanger that last special lock of hair—his last few strands.

"You aren't getting too rough with her, are you?"

"She started it. She likes it."

"I see," I say.

I do not add that it wouldn't be the way that I would play with her. I've never seen a woman play with a baby the way a man does. Ring toss, baby toss, growl and yank. These rough and tumble games aren't recommended in the books on child care that I read, and frankly, I don't know why not—the kid eats them up.

The Bride-to-Be In Her Bath

"I wish you wouldn't bathe the baby in the sink when it's threatening to rain," my father said.

"Where do you think I should bathe Katie?" my sister Patty asked.

"Why bathe her at all? How dirty could she be? It's not like she works for a living," Dad opined.

"I'm going to bathe the baby," Patty stated flatly. "I promise I won't use up the hot water."

"It's not the hot water I'm worried about. I'm afraid the baby will be struck by lightning while you're bathing her."

"Inside the house? In the sink? Before it even starts to rain?"

Dad shrugged off the implicit criticism. "It could happen. Water attracts lightning."

"I'll put my body between the window and Katie," the daughter this man used to call Princess promised. "If lightning strikes, it will hit me first."

That thought seemed to comfort my father temporarily; but after a moment, he argued, "But your hands will be wet, and you'll be holding my Precious Love."

"I promise that my body will absorb most of the electricity," Katie's mother said, gamely turning on the faucet.

Seeing that the baby was going to be bathed over his protestations, Dad suggested, "Well, at least stand on the rug. It has a rubber bottom. Maybe that will help."

This conversation is typical of the child care discussions that take place around the newest grandchild.

Katie has brought out all of my father's nervousness about the pitfalls of baby-raising, and these parental caveats range from how to bathe Katie to taking the child to the mall, where, in her stroller, this innocent victim, according to my father's view, is forced to breathe dust kicked up by shoppers.

"Why do you want to put a perfectly clean baby in the path of people and their miserable dirty feet?" Dad asked when Patty and Katie headed off to the mall last Saturday.

"We have to go somewhere," my sister said.

"Why?"

"Because the baby can't just stay here all the time."

"Why?"

"Because she finds other people interesting."

"Why?"

"I don't know why she likes other people. Katie is a social child. She likes to mingle."

"I think you're speaking for yourself and projecting onto the baby," my father theorized, stroking his chin thoughtfully.

Dad has picked up the word "projecting" from one of the talk shows. Dad's only previous experience with projecting has been the old-fashioned kind, when he showed those home movies of my three sisters and me waving at the camera, though we were never really going anywhere.

My sister stifles a retort, for she has studied psychology, and she knows what's happening here. Our Pa is an anxious grandfather, obsessively cautious about the child he has dubbed Precious Love, daughter of the girl he always called Princess.

After the bath, Patty pushed the baby off in the stroller for a turn in the park. Our Pa stood at the window and watched his Princess and his Precious Love leave the safety of his fortress. His was a somber farewell speech: "I can't believe a child of mine would be fool enough to take the baby to the park. Think of the wild dogs that could be prowling, the squirrels that could be rabid, strangers with germs on their hands touching the swings that the baby will hold, and then she'll put her hands in her mouth. Not to mention all that dirt. God, please help her."

Daddy prays out loud to God, who He knows always hears him. He thinks that we don't.

"Katie will be fine," I promised him.

He looked at me with a fresh suspicion. "Sometimes, I don't know what to make of your sister."

I did. And being her sister, I attempted to deflect some of our father's anxiety from her to me. I confessed softly, "I took Katie to the grocery store this morning."

Before he could launch into his warnings about the dangers lurking at Foodworld, lightning flashed across the sky and jagged threateningly toward the Village Green park. Thunder boomed. The neighborhood dogs began to howl. In my mind, I saw them gather, those wild, howling potentially rabid beasts, and head off in a stormy herd to the park, where they would attack and devour the innocent children playing there. Or, maybe this time our Precious Love would be struck by lightning.

I had meant to comfort my father–perhaps in time, to reason with him. Instead, I took my place beside him at the front door, and together we watched for the children to come home.

THE BRIDE-TO-BE AT HOME WITH HER AUNT

My mother has shed ten pounds since she started keeping her new grandbaby every day. "A new baby can really take the weight off of you," she explains archly.

Because I am a chunky girl who could stand to lose ten pounds, my mother thinks that if I see some personal reward in baby-sitting, I will be more willing to continue taking a turn keeping Katie.

"Yes, taking care of a little baby is better than an aerobic workout, and you do not even know you are doing it. The pounds just melt away," Mother adds, sighing with contentment.

This pitch is as hard-sell as it's going to get. My mother does not believe in pressuring; she holds out her reasons and lets me decide. The pitch is effective. For even though I love being with my new niece, I don't mind the idea of shedding a pound or two. Indeed, inspired by my mother's own weight loss, I have lately been choosing low-cal lunches to complement the baby-care workout.

"You are looking wonderful," I assure my mother, and she does. Her complexion is rosy; her face is thinner. She is more agile than she has been in years.

See Grandmother scoop up baby. See Grandmother snap open new diaper with one hand. See Baby Katie all fresh and clean.

Daddy interrupted Mother. "It only takes three adults standing on their heads all day long to keep one little baby girl happy."

"It does not," Mother argues.

Katie holds out chubby eager arms to me and coos, "Oh, most favorite aunt, come and take me to your world where everything is an adventure."

"If you will pack me a bag, I'll take the baby to my house for the afternoon. Her mama can pick her up there. You could get some rest," I offer casually. "You might even take a nap."

"A nap?" Mama asks, her left eye twitching hopefully. "That does sound nice."

"In your bed, on the couch, on Katie's pallet. It is entirely up to you. Of course you won't be exercising. Those pounds might start to creep back on. I'd hate to thwart your progress," I add devilishly.

"Women my age need a little weight on them. Don't worry about me," she counters quickly, assembling some bottles and diapers in the bag. As much as she loves me and the baby, I am out of there in two minutes flat with Katie slapped on my hip. We're barely settled at home before the telephone rings. It's Katie's mother, who works full-time as a legal secretary and misses Katie all day long.

"Are you all right?" Patty asks. Her voice is low, concerned.

"We're both doing fine. Katie is safely on the pallet watching ***Kitty Foyle.***"

When I speak, my niece nods to me that ***Kitty Foyle*** *is a four-star movie just like I said it was. Then, she turns her attention back to Ginger Rogers, who has fallen in love with the wrong man.*

"If you want to bring her downtown for lunch, I'll buy. The place up the street has a dessert cart with only chocolate on it. The food is fabulous. I'll buy you anything you want."

"Not today," I say. I find it ironic that my mother promises weight loss if I will keep Katie, while my sister attempts to reward me with food when I do. "My hair is dirty, and I'm not dressed. We'll come another day," I promise. I know my sister must be missing her child, and I vow privately to make it up to her with as many lunches as we can work out in the future.

On the pallet with Katie, I hold out my arms. She crawls up on top of me and lays her head on my chest. We watch the movie peacefully. The time eases by. I enjoy having my day elongated. I did not know being with a child slowed down time.

Katie brings this gift of time that no one has told me about. In gratitude, I tell Katie that Ginger Rogers is also a dancer. " Ginger is most famous for dancing with Fred Astaire, but she did a great deal more than that. It's a sad fact-of-life that many talented, accomplished women are still only recognized for what they did in the company of a man. I think that Ginger Rogers won the Oscar for playing this role, and you notice that Fred is not even in this movie."

During the commercials, we walk over to the picture window, and I point out squirrels, rabbits, and terrapins. I introduce her to the piano and show her which hands go where. She rejoices in sounds. Next, I play my answering machine tape three times so that she can hear her mother's voice. She grows solemn, and I wonder what she feels and thinks and what it will be like when she has a vocabulary that can reveal her personhood.

An hour later, we sigh together when Ginger Rogers gives up that man who caused her so much trouble and chooses the right man after all.

"You don't have to get married to be happy, Katie," I say. "But if you are going to fall in love, it is best to choose a man who likes to work and thinks of other people besides himself." She is too young to hear about heartbreak so I ask her, "What shall we watch next?"

Katie tears off the top page of the ***TV Guide*** *in response.*

"How about Perry Mason? Now there's a man who's smart and loyal and helpful to his clients and friends, but you will notice in time that he's been stringing his secretary Della Street along for years. You have to watch out for that kind of man. Perry Mason cannot seem to make a romantic commitment."

Before the program begins, I feed her a warm jar of carrots and offer her a secret forbidden sip of Coca-Cola. She presses the cold glass against her sore teething gums and slaps me on the head with her fist in gratitude. I kiss her face; she holds mine.

The phone rings. It's my mother. "Are you all right?" she asks intently. "I haven't heard from you, and I was getting worried."

"The pounds are just melting away," I promise her. "I'm perfectly fine, really," I assure her. "Go rest your hands and feet some more."

"You're being awfully good," she whispers wonderingly, and hangs up.

Back on the pallet, I ask Katie, "Aren't we being good?"

She brings her nose to my face and flutters her eye lashes against my cheek.

"Ah, butterfly love," I grin, batting my eyes in response. "But not too much exercise though. We don't want to get too thin." She laughs.

Perry Mason finally comes on. I tell Katie that her mother works in a law office. "She is a legal secretary like Della Street. It's a tough job. Not everyone can do it. She works there to get your health insurance and to have the money to feed you and buy your diapers. Your mother loves you very much. Probably more than I do."

I'm not sure how that is possible, but it must be true. During the commercials, I explain to Katie how the legal system works in America. It's very possible that she is the brightest child who was ever born, for she understands every word I say.

The Bride-to-Be Shares Her Dream of Heaven

I am on hug restriction today with my niece Katie, who has outgrown my possessive embraces and some of the decisions I still try to make for her, like what she should order at lunch. At the cafeteria when the server behind the buffet line asks, "Does she want the child's plate?" I nod almost imperceptibly, because although my niece doesn't think of herself as a child, I do.

Intent on making sure she gets blue Jell-O, nine-year-old Katie hurriedly orders fried chicken, ignoring the fact that they place a fat chicken thigh on her plate and she will eat only chicken legs. I say nothing because she might think this is one of those instances when I am smothering her, and as a consequence, embarrassing her.

We move carefully down the line, holding up as much traffic in the cafeteria as I do in the car.

Katie and I move carefully to the check-out, where the cashier rings for a waiter to help us get to a table. I can carry my tray, but Katie can't manage hers. She accepts the offer of a waiter's help more readily than she can accept mine.

I do not hurry to go back after her, stealing looks over my shoulder instead to see if she can handle talking with the waiter who is appointed to carry her tray. When she joins me at the table, she suggests matter-of-factly, "If I placed my drink on your tray, I could carry my own tray. It's the drink that I can't balance."

I nod thoughtfully, tipping the waiter a dollar. "That's a good idea. We'll do that next time."

In spite of our growing pains, we are having a good day, and I am already looking ahead to another day with Katie, another lunch, another time to look into her old-soul liquid green eyes and connect with the girl who is the last part of my parents that I still have to enjoy.

I see her that way sometimes. Other times, she is a little kid, a young lady, my sister's daughter, and prissy the way her mother was at nine. I smile thinking of my prissy sister who gave us this newest child to love. And just as I am in the midst of an old maiden aunt's reveries I spy a man who looks just like my Uncle Sammy, who has been in heaven a long time now.

"Do you see that man?" I say, pointing over Katie's shoulder. "He looks just like your Uncle Sammy. Did you ever meet him?" It is strange to have become the family historian. I often ruminate about people who aren't here anymore. I am happy to tell the stories of people who are a part of the family tree, but they are strangers who live only in these stories for Katie and her generation.

"Maybe I met him," Katie says politely. "I don't eat chicken thighs. I eat only chicken legs," she says, looking puzzled. 'How did you slip up?' She wonders. She eyes me curiously, as if I am a stranger.

I smile. I see that I am not supposed to hug her, but I am supposed to monitor her chicken dinner. I am learning the ever-evolving rules of how independence feels to her and how her expectations limit mine.

I send back the chicken thigh, not caring if it will cost more. Wouldn't I give her the moon if I could and certainly a chicken leg?

I do not say this out loud any more than I permit myself to hug her up tightly at the very thought that she never met Uncle Sammy, a rather splendid fellow who loved us and was very good at playing the game of Trivial Pursuit. He and I were always paired on family game nights, and we made a formidable team. That's not very important information, but it seems sacred somehow in this moment.

"Your grandmother really loved Sammy," I said, moving past the memory to another one. "My mother loved all her brothers, but she had a special place in her heart for her brother Sammy."

"I miss grandmother," Katie confessed as the chicken leg arrived. She dove upon it with the appetite that I enjoy seeing. I am hoping she will want another chicken leg so I can buy it for her.

"I had a dream about Uncle Sammy," I said. "It was right after he left us to go and be with God. In my dream he was in a small cottage that was covered in a sheet of something that looked like ice but it wasn't cold and it seemed lit up from within, kind of like holy ice, pure. I like to think the dream was a picture of heaven, and I could only see through the picture window, because I am still here. Uncle Sammy looked very happy in that dream—happier in ways that one can only imagine this side of heaven."

For a second I remembered what the dream felt like, to stand outside and look in and be glad that he who had suffered with cancer was smiling now. I did not talk about cancer or death, however, for this child has seen almost as much as I have.

"I dreamed of heaven once," Katie said nonchalantly, picking up a square of blue Jell-O. She eats this as prissily as her mother once upon a time ate dill pickles. Katie eats Jell-O squares with her fingers, her pinkie raised, the image incongruously ladylike and kidlike. I cast myself ahead to the future where I, in my role as family historian, will be telling someone about Katie and the adorable way she ate blue Jell-O squares.

"And what was heaven like in your dream?" I asked, scooping a forkful of black-eyed peas.

"All the houses were made of sunflowers and it snowed, but the snow was like glitter—not cold. Pretty. Falling all over me," she said simply, shaking her hair as if to let the snowflakes fly.

"And did you see anyone you loved there?" I prompted.

"Oh, yes," she admitted. "I saw every dog I've ever loved. I saw Rufus, Luke, and Gatsby. They were all there."

"You saw dogs in heaven?" I probed.

"All the dogs I've ever loved," Katie said, nodding seriously. She stopped to take a long sip of cola.

I drank water and sighed. "I don't suppose you saw any people in heaven in your dream?" I prompted.

"Oh, yes," as if people in heaven was an afterthought.

"The whole family is there," she said. "You are there," she said, using the present tense in a way that makes an English teacher uncomfortable but an Aunt very happy.

I stopped inside the stillness of her dream for that moment and saw love-ever-after dreamed of through a child's eyes: we were there already somehow but we were going there too, and it was a place where all the dogs and people I've ever loved are and ever will be.

"And when I woke up," Katie said, old soul eyes gleaming, small girl fingers touching blue Jell-O, "I laughed.

The Bride-to-Be Goes Shopping

Her small handprints mar the glass surface of the grocery's deli case. The deli manager frowns at the fingertips which trill across the glass, first here, then there.

"Katie," I say. "The lady just cleaned the glass. Don't touch it again."

Katie pirouettes over to me. "May I have a piece of that ham to eat right now?" she asks expectantly. Her smile is sunny. Her greenish eyes peer up bright and with a hint of laughter in them. Her thick brown hair is plaited on either side, and she is wearing a green bandanna that she found in the back seat of the car on the drive over here. She immediately tied the cloth on her head to make a fashion statement.

"You can have some ham once we're in the car, although I could make you a whole sandwich at home," I prompt.

"Why not right now?"

"Not right now," I say, shaking my head, as we take our pound of deli ham and head toward the dairy case for milk.

My 10-year old niece doesn't walk to the next destination. She skips, while her hands move through the air as she practices over and over a movement that I can't place as part of a dance routine. A volleyball move? Basketball?

It is probably some dance move that Jennifer Lopez made popular with girls my niece's age. I like Jennifer Lopez, too, but I don't like her as much as my niece does who, upon being asked to write a story for English class, instantly contrived a fantasy scenario where she and J. Lo went shopping in the mall together. Katie read the story to me over fresh Krispy Kreme doughnuts Saturday morning, her glasses falling forward on her nose while she spoke aloud the envisioned fantasy of a great day of shopping with J. Lo.

"Good," I said, nodding.

My praise sent her downward over the paper to write nine more words. She counted them for me, her fingers moving across the page, feeling the words.

"Good job," I repeat, ruffling her hair with my hand. She is accustomed to my hands trailing her features, tousling her sun-kissed hair when it isn't plaited, and when it is.

I like every style of hers.

"We need 2% milk," I say, hoping to distract her.

Katie skips up to the case and finds a gallon, peering deep inside the case to check the date. Using both arms she carries the milk to our buggy, her body taking note of the feel of it against her chest. She grins in delight and says, wonderingly, "Cold."

"Thank you," I say, as she lowers it clumsily into the buggy, for there is only one kind of movement for taking out groceries and putting them in: clumsy. Grocery shopping is not a ballet.

I lean on the buggy, glad for its support, though I chide myself that I am too often now shifting into the posture of leaning on whatever is nearby. My niece does not know this type of self-consciousness yet. Her hands and feet work better than when she just began to walk and touch and bumble along on legs learning to stand. Most things she reached for went right to her mouth.

The germs! The germs! It has been my warning– my lament– for years, but so far fear of germs hasn't taken root in this young girl who hurriedly pulls the buggy to the check-out for we are on our way to volleyball practice. She played basketball last year. She is steadily moving through different sports to see if any of them will stick as one that she is particularly attuned to–gifted in.

We stand in the check-out line. Her fingers trace the names of candy bars in the rack. She points to a Snickers bar, her favorite, and I nod, discreetly. She encroaches on the personal space of the shopper in front of us to grab it. Holding it, she closes her eyes and moans, "Chocolate." She will place it on the conveyor belt, and once it is scanned, retrieve it immediately. She can't eat it until after lunch, but she will hold onto it until then.

While waiting, she adjusts her bandanna and examines the phone cards that are hanging mostly over the head of the cashier. Nearby shoppers wait for me to tell her to be still– to learn the posture of stillness and self-containment that leads, I see, to leaning on buggies.

I suddenly see people like me as the enemy of the young and the energetic. Rather than rebuke her, I censor myself. I pull a piece of ham from the cellophane bag and hand it to her wordlessly. Delighted, she stuffs it in her mouth.

I ignore the unspoken criticism of others nearby and work on standing upright. I can do it. The leaning is a habit I've drifted into, and I shouldn't have.

The poses of maturity often lead to this kind of inhibited posture. We tell others to be afraid of germs, to stay still, to stay hungry until you can do something more polite about it until we grow too still and stay hungry too long. Even being in a grocery store doesn't tempt us out of leaning on the maxims of constraining ourselves and others. We don't just nag others; we nag ourselves and call it the wisdom of delayed gratification. The adventure of being alive should not be buried under the rules of "wait, don't touch, don't taste, don't dance right now."

Giving up dancing isn't wise, and growing older shouldn't be this still.

J. Lo knows it and so does my niece. In that very moment I grew up, and I decided I agreed with them.

The Bride-to-Be and Figuring Time

When the rain clouds form, I wonder where Katie is and if she's okay. She probably is. I am more afraid of her being afraid of storms than she is, really.

But when the winds pick up and the day turns suddenly dark, I flinch, holding back the impulse to go up and down the streets looking for her. She's in summer camp at the Y.

That's where she is all right. Where the pool is. And they swim in the mornings and again in the afternoons, I think. She'll be brown as a nut, and her hair will be as blond as it can get. That Katie! In my mind she still runs on the legs of a toddler but in truth, she is almost as tall as I am. Her legs may be even longer than mine.

Tall for her age, her height declares that she has lived longer than she really has. Ten years old is not that old. Compare it to dog years or cat years or even rat years (she likes rats) and it's still ten years old, human time.

But human time is not so easy to figure any more. The pace of technology pushes us to move faster than our legs can carry us–not faster than our thoughts can take us, but sometimes emotions don't adjust to an idea as fast as a brain can. There's a strange balance to seek. There is a heart adjustment to the progression of time lived out in children, who upon learning of our fears for them, actually laugh at us.

My sister's children do that. She told me so. Julie said that since her children have scattered to different time zones, she is always trying to place them in the schedule of their days while she is living out hers. She lives with them this way only under different roofs. "I'm up at 7; they're up at 8. We eat at different times, later now for us on Eastern Standard Time."

But there is more to this sense of being late than living in a time zone that means all her favorite TV shows are on an hour later than Julie wants to watch them. Julie yawns through ***Law & Order*** *now, calculating when her distant babies will go to bed: that married daughter, her son in med school, and her youngest son heads to college in the fall, but not another literal time zone, just the time zone of a young man who will be keeping on-my-own college hours rather than under-mother's-roof hours.*

Julie knows what I mean. She figures time like I do. One eye on the clock, her mind trails the streets and other rooms where her grown children live–those places where we can't keep an eye on them so we keep an eye on the clock, figuring time.

"You're always doing that," her daughter Jan laughed. "Figuring time like that."

Ben agreed. "Everything gets compared to something else."

They think their mother is just a clock watcher. It's more than that. She's a mother who measures out her days in more than minutes; she measures them in the footsteps of growing children who walk beyond her vision. They live in cities where she doesn't always know when the clouds gather or the sky grows suddenly gray. Rather, she waits to hear a weather report from them at week's end. When they tell her about the heat and the rain and the times when they needed an umbrella, she sees them in a different way than the way they tell of their days. She sees them the way I see Katie every day while she's at camp or in her rat science class.

Mothers and aunts and fathers too figure time by a different instrument–the human heart. It's not as fast as technology, but it is truer way of figuring time than any man-made timepiece.

The Bride-to-Be Becomes Herself

Although I arrive early to meet her as she gets out of school, the sight of her still surprises me. I can't immediately pick Katie out of the rushing crowd of other school children her size, and although I was with her in the morning when she chose the ensemble she is wearing, I don't really recognize her right away. Katie is a blur of denim and T-shirt, hair in a loose pony tail, and she is wearing wire-rim eye glasses, as nearsighted now as I was at her age.

The glasses give her a scholarly appearance, which reflects the truth of her inclinations and abilities born of curiosity and discipline.

"Can we get a strawberry smoothie?" she asks, as I embrace her this new way. It is the embrace of tolerance, endurance. Sometimes I feel that she is waiting for me to outgrow my immature idea of her as the baby, which is what I still call her.

"Sure, Baby," I say, wondering if her aversion to the name is more serious than I know.

"That's him," she says, walking ahead of me toward the car. Her long-legged gait challenges me to keep up with her, and the tilt of her head, the jut of her chin, speak independence and the growing self-possession of a young girl not so young that she hasn't identified the first crush of her life.

I glance behind me at the tall young man who is two years older than my niece, and I see and say what I always say when she reports the presence of this 13-year-old boy all the girls love. "He is really cute."

I wonder if my language is as out-of-date as I am in other ways. Should I say he's a doll, a man's man, a honey-bunny? I don't like that word hot—not at all. It speaks only of sexuality, and there is so much more to being attractive than the tension of physical chemistry.

I'm pretty sure that the words of admiration that spring to my mind as accolades of admiration for this really cute guy are not the language of love for her generation, her age, both real and imagined. But I do not know those words now. I didn't know very many of them when I was her age either.

He's not her boyfriend; he's a possibility and a picture too of the physical type of man she most likely will be attracted to. Today, she likes a blond guy with an air of self-assurance that my niece has as well.

She can walk into a room with a sense of belonging that only comes upon me from time to time, depending on the position of the moon, my hormones, and whether I feel five pounds lighter.

I find a $10 bill, and we drive toward the strawberry smoothie shop.

"Isn't it lovely that the store is so convenient?' she inquires in an overly formal tone that mimics my own.

'Do I sound like that?' I am both flattered and disturbed that her mirroring of me is so accurate.

"Indeed," I reply, handing her the money. "I don't want one today. I have a strawberry pie made at home, and I don't want to ruin my appetite for it," I explain.

"I've never seen a strawberry pie," she remarks wonderingly, surprised that there are things as simple as a certain kind of pie that she doesn't know about.

"Perhaps you would like a piece," I prompt, my tone of voice an uncanny imitation of her imitation of me.

She smiles tolerantly, looking out the window. The landscape of strip shopping centers passes by.

When I used to pick up my niece from day school, the view of the landscape was different: cows, pastures, a Christmas tree farm. I collected her each afternoon, taking the route that caught the afternoon sunlight in a way that created the illusion of stars on the interior ceiling of the car.

"You can reach for the stars," I used to tell her, when she was dazzled by the light.

Then her plump baby hands would reach up and wave, attempting to catch the dancing light of star shapes, and she always laughed. She laughed every time, every day.

Now, she reaches for the stars on her own. I don't always see how she does it–this long-legged girl with a crush on a blond boy, and that's even better. I don't always recognize every expression, and I can't read her mind with the facility of someone who shares the intimacies of constant daily converse, and I miss it, but the sacrifice of sharing a string of moments in her life so that she can gain the independence I see in her today–this little stranger–is worth absolutely everything.

The Bride-to-Be Goes to College

As you prepare to go to college I think about what I need to say to you as you head out the door. I know you heard me about being leery of bald-headed men who drive convertibles and don't have enough sense to wear a hat, and I know you heard me when I pointed out that man jogging around the neighborhood in his underwear and the implications of both his self-possession and our response to his comfort level of exposed vulnerability in front of strangers (us). We decided he posed one of those questions that we don't need to answer.

He is, Katie. That man jogging in his underwear is emblematic of many oddities in life that do not require you to make sense of them.

Let the memory of him remind you to turn your attention to the questions relevant right now for you on a college campus.

For the most part I have left the questions about romance and religion to your mother, except for those occasions when you have asked me a direct question about my own faith. I have told you the truth about Jesus. What you need to remember always is that he is real. Although you will be going to college where they teach you questions and offer you often pat answers about the creation of life and its meaning, I can tell you that while the experience of college will be exhilarating in its open-ended exploration of the best ideas that men and women can come up with, there are many paths that lead nowhere in particular. Some ideas require no more serious cogitation than that man jogging by us in his underwear did.

You've heard of wilderness experiences from the Old Testament. Sometimes the freedom to explore tantalizing questions doesn't turn out to be discovery at all—sometimes, those experiences are mainly circuitous meanderings– wilderness experiences where the explorer wanders around looking at various strange trees, believing that by knowing the number of trees, time spent in wandering, and the amount of money spent on text books and tuition that you are going somewhere that will ultimately be validated as meaningful or a destination called progress. Sometimes, the only real measure of that experience is that you survived it, but you don't always learn something distinctively true and life or faith enhancing.

A big subject in college that often leads to a wilderness experience is the blanket assertion by scientific thinkers and logic advocates that evolution disproves the supremacy of God as the creator of you and this planet. Evolution is a wonderful dynamic to explore. It's true, by the way. But it does not disprove that God made everything. He made the dynamic of evolution. To me, evolution's most tantalizing feature is the creative dynamic of natural selection upon which an understanding of evolution is based. You can look at the scientific evidence and agree with what you see, but it does not disprove that God made everything. You will need a different faculty in yourself to know this, and it won't be reason alone, although, ideally, reason can take you there eventually, my dear. You will need to trust that part of your curiosity that is fused with imagination and which explores what reason alone cannot—you will need to let your soul keep company with the Holy Spirit of God and allow him to lead you into all truth. Jesus says that he will, and he will, because Jesus does not and cannot lie. You will follow the history of dates and changes in human kind and animal life, and depending upon how far you pursue the investigation, you will find interesting data about the intersection of viruses on human life and the small big bangs of jumping genes as they inform our understanding of the human genome. You will encounter many big words, beautifully constructed paradigms of science, and also philosophy and poetry, but you will never get to the root of an explanation for why we humans are here that is more tantalizing or true than God created us for himself so that he could have someone to love. And then he waits for us to love him, and he asks us in excruciatingly tender ways to love one another.

Because we are paradoxically attracted to and terrified of being loved intimately and completely, we tend to leave or try to hide from God, so he sent Jesus to first find us and then explain Love to us again. Jesus didn't leave us orphans when he finished his work here. The Holy Spirit uses the intellectual advances of humankind to hint at aspects of God-Is-Love's nature, but never mistake the ideas of men for the absolute truth about God or Jesus or the Holy Spirit.

Even the very best preachers only come close occasionally to getting this right. By this, I mean, the characterization of the nature of eternal love that is possible right now in communion with God which happens only because the Great Lover of Mankind (and Creator of it, too) has made this communion possible. Your soul intersects with the Holy Spirit. In the Bible, this is referred to as tabernacling. That gift fits inside what we call grace, and it means that God makes everything that is good that can happen between us possible.

To begin to experience grace, we simply have to believe God and put him first. Anything that comes before our love for him is what he calls an idol.

I suspect that because I have always called you Beloved and you have rightly signed your cards to me that way, you believe that I have made you into an idol of sorts. There have been times when I felt you resisting my love because it was oppressive to you; I know it has been. Unconditional love can feel like that to others, but it is not intended that way. I have loved you unconditionally, and you have never been an idol to me. You have always been only a gift from God. But do you see how big that is—you, Katie Ellen, a gift from God?

I greatly admire you, Katie, my Beloved. Most of the times I only tell you this in ways that you are used to hearing—pretty hair, pretty face. But I see you much more deeply than that, and I know you are an authentic human being who is only temporarily seventeen and works at a pet store where you do not find the task of cleaning up pet poop beneath you. I admire that—as I enjoy how often you come home wanting to buy one of the dogs that you are responsible for showing to others. It must be difficult to function something like a person in an adoption agency who must try and find needy animals homes and to make judgments (and how can we help it?) in that moment about whether the prospective parents—your store's customers– are good enough to raise the animals you already love.

As you weigh and assess the dangers of your customers becoming the parents of the dogs you love, think of how I must consider trusting you to strangers to raise—people like college teachers who are bound by their own pressures, driven by their own egos, and biased by questions that have haunted them all their lives and for which they are still looking for answers and may try to justify their inclinations and their answers by telling you information that isn't always true. They don't usually know they're lying. They don't usually know they have denied the truth of God because they are afraid of being completely and deeply loved by God. They can't believe that. I know this is true mainly because I am a college teacher and some of my friends are people who are afraid of unconditional love. Sometimes I am, too, still. I am as capable of being fearful and wrong as anyone, and I regularly monitor myself to make sure that I am not trying to justify my faith at the expense of people who don't believe as I do and don't want to. They have that right. It's called free will, and I respect it without reservation.

Ultimately, as you begin your studies in college and soon declare yourself in a field of study, be happy and enjoy that pursuit, but the most open-ended intellectual and spiritual pursuit of yours or anyone's life is the continued worship of and longing for Jesus and more of Him. Listen carefully at college, and as you hear invitations to think about all kinds of ways that people organize meaning out of human experience, remember that all of them have an end. All of them have a conclusion.

You are about to go and see more of the world than I can control, and I don't want to. The adventure is thrilling. But there is far more to being alive than learning the pieces of puzzles that fit inside a cerebral paradigm. There is life itself, and that happens inside the living love of the Resurrected Savior whose ongoing mission is to keep talking to the Father about us, and all the while he is calling to us, whispering, beckoning, waiting. He is there, is my point. He lives. Live with him and the puzzles of cerebral enterprises find a different place in what you value, and when you do, you are more alive, more thrilled, more free than in any other kind of simple thinking. You are going off to college, and it is quite an adventure; but you will never find a greater adventure than following the Shepherd who will not lead you astray or unto any kind of death that you need ever fear. Let every day begin with his name on your lips as you ask him to keep you company, and let every day end with gratitude for what he has given you, for he gives you your very life. As he has given me mine.

I cannot give you life or much more than words of encouragement like these as you go off to college. In this world I have mainly been a college teacher, and I can only speak of what it is like on campus and what I have seen and what I can remember from my own days of venturing out.

I can imagine much. But I know this: God loves you, Jesus is real, the Bible tells the truth, and if you would work on your penmanship and take care to use it when you are writing those essay exams in your college classes, your grades will shoot up.

Beloved....

When I began assembling this collection of recipes for you I revisited Miss Esther's recipe box and identified the dishes I thought might interest you. You may recall that Miss Esther had a recipe for living. It was a prayer and a declaration. "Every day is a good day."

But you have to make it a good day.

She also said that if you were feeling discouraged, you had to encourage yourself. "Give yourself a boost when no one else will." Because you will be spending time alone as a military wife, you will need to remember that recipe for getting through stretches of time when you are lonely and needing a boost. You will also need to have some recipes at hand. Here are the selected recipes from Miss Esther's recipe box.

As I sifted through two boxes of recipes from Miss Esther to select some for you, it occurred to me that cooks don't have to collect recipes like this anymore. They are out there in a virtual world and can be called up and recalled with a few clicks of the keyboard. You will be doing that, I'm sure, and I have done that, too, finding recipes that I have enjoyed and trusted would be there.

More often, I print them out and modify them to fit my taste. (I have done this with my Butter Pecan Cake recipe.)

But when people sift through my drawers and boxes they won't find a collection of recipes the way Miss Esther kept hers and which tell a pretty interesting story of her life on a farm. They will simply find the kind of cookies that are electronic, not made with eggs and butter.

I like the speed and breadth of access to recipes online, but there is a problem with seeing dishes to make this way that parallels a problem I have seen in myself from time to time, and I have seen it in others too. It is when the idea of a dish or an idea of a project to complete feels more real than it is because it exists on the Internet and in their thoughts. Here, the virtual world intersects with the imagined world, and in a strange way, they share a common problem. Imagining that you can do something is not the same validation and fulfillment as actually doing something. Many people are self-deceived by the activity of thinking about something—a kind of collecting of ideas the way some people collect recipes—but they don't actually ever make the dish.

A big difference between Miss Esther and other kinds of cooks is that she collected recipes and made the dishes. Others collect recipes and never make the dishes but talk about the recipes as if they have been kitchen-tested and family approved.

Be careful to see yourself clearly as you navigate a brick-and-mortar world while visiting the virtual world of the Internet. One kind of experience matters more than the other kind. Make sure you know the difference when you collect your own set of instructions and recipes for creating the best home life possible.

Section 9

EVERY DAY IS A GOOD DAY—RECIPES FROM MISS ESTHER

What's in this section:

Esther's Handed-Down Chicken and Dumplings

Esther's Pimiento Cheese Sandwich Spread

Esther's Applesauce Cake

Esther's Basic Apple Pie

Esther's Chocolate Sheath Cake

Esther's French Fudge

Esther's Gingerbread

Esther's Pecan Cake

A Taste of Home: *Riding with the windows down, living with the windows open*

Miss Esther's Recipes

Miss Esther's Handed-Down Chicken and Dumplings

Ingredients:

2 cups flour

1 teaspoon baking powder

1 teaspoon salt

1 cup shortening

½ cup liquid (¼ cup water and ¼ cup milk)

A stewed chicken

Directions:

Combine dry ingredients. Cut in shortening.

Add liquid. Roll on a floured board until paper thin. Cut into smallest strips possible. Drop into kettle of stewed chicken. Cover and cook 8 to 10 minutes.

Miss Esther's Pimiento Cheese Sandwich Spread

Ingredients:

1 14 oz. can of evaporated milk

1 pound of American cheese, grated—sharp cheddar is good.

2 tablespoons vinegar

½ teaspoon dry mustard

1 7-ounce jar of pimientos chopped (buy them chopped)

½ teaspoon salt

Dash of cayenne pepper

Directions:

Heat milk in double boiler.

Add cheese. Stir until melted.

Cool.

Add other ingredients and stir until smooth.

Store in refrigerator.

If you like, you can add a little grated onion or chopped scallion.

Miss Esther's Applesauce Cake

Ingredients:

½ cup shortening

1 cup sugar

1 ½ cups sweetened applesauce

1 cup raisins

1 cup dates

1 teaspoon nutmeg

1 teaspoon cinnamon

1 teaspoon allspice

2 ½ cups flour

1 teaspoon soda

1 tablespoon hot water

1 cup chopped nuts

Directions:

Blend shortening, sugar, and ½ cup applesauce. Add the fruit. Sift spices with flour and add alternately with remaining cup of applesauce. Combine soda with hot water and add to the mixture. Add the nuts. Bake in a tube or loaf pan 1 hour at 350 degrees.

You can add this glaze if you want to: Combine and bring to a rolling boil ½ cup white corn syrup and ¼ cup water. Cool until lukewarm and pour over the cake.

Miss Esther's Basic Apple Pie

Ingredients:

1 egg

1 ½ cups sugar

1 stick margarine or butter

1 teaspoon cinnamon

3 cups chopped apples

2 pie shells

Directions:

Mix ingredients together. Put the mixture in an unbaked pie shell that you have pierced several times with the tongs of a fork. Cover with another pie shell.

Make five slits in top of pie to vent the steam.

Add a dusting of sugar to make it pretty.

Bake at 350 degrees until brown.

Chocolate Sheath Cake

Ingredients and directions for the cake:

Put 2 cups sugar and 2 cups flour in a bowl and set aside (mixed up).

Then, in a saucepan, put:

1 stick margarine

½ cup Crisco

4 tablespoons cocoa

1 cup water.

Mix well and bring to a rapid boil. Stir well. Remove from the heat, and add the sugar and flour mixture.

Then, add ½ cup buttermilk, two slightly beaten eggs, a teaspoon of soda, and a teaspoon of vanilla extract. Bake in a greased pan at 400 degrees for 20 minutes.

Icing:

About five minutes before the cake is done, mix one stick of margarine, 3 tablespoons cocoa, 6 tablespoons of milk. Mix and melt together and bring to a rapid boil. Remove from the heat. Add 1 box of powdered sugar and a teaspoon of vanilla extract plus a cup of chopped pecans.

Spread on the cake while it is hot.

Miss Esther's French Fudge

Ingredients:

1 package (6 oz.) semi-sweet chocolate pieces

⅓ cup PLUS 1 tablespoon Eagle Brand Sweetened Condensed Milk

Pinch of salt

½ teaspoon Vanilla extract

Directions:

Heat chocolate in double-boiler top over fast-boiling water, stirring until just melted.

Remove from heat.

Add Eagle Brand condensed milk (or any brand), salt, vanilla extract, and nuts.

Stir until smooth. Turn onto wax-paper-lined contained and press into block one inch high.

Chill in refrigerator until firm, about 2 hours.

Makes ½ pound of smooth fudge.

P. S. And, no, I do not know what makes it French fudge.

Esther's Gingerbread

Ingredients:

½ cup butter and some shortening mixed

½ cup sugar

1 egg

1 cup molasses

2 ½ cups flour

1 ½ teaspoons soda

1 teaspoon ground cinnamon

1 teaspoon ground ginger

½ teaspoon ground cloves

½ teaspoon salt

1 cup of hot water.

Directions:

Using an electric mixer, cream the shortening and sugar. Add the beaten egg and the molasses. Add the dry ingredients which have been mixed. Add the hot water and beat until smooth.

Bake in a shallow loaf pan (13 x 9 x 2) at 350 degrees about forty minutes.

Miss Esther's Pecan Cake

Ingredients:

4 eggs

2 cups sugar

1 cup shortening (butter, margarine, lard)

3 cups flour

1 teaspoon baking powder

1 teaspoon soda

1 teaspoon ground cinnamon

1 teaspoon ground cloves

1 cup of buttermilk

2 cups chopped pecans

Make it this way.

Beat eggs. Add sugar and shortening. Add the dry ingredients and milk alternately and beat well. Add pecans. Bake in a greased tube pan at 350 degrees for one hour.

A Taste of Home....

RIDING WITH THE WINDOWS DOWN, LIVING WITH THE WINDOWS OPEN

In the South in the summertime you don't usually ride in the car with the windows down. You would be breathing steam heat, a kind of muggy air that would drown the uninitiated.

Because the summers and summerlike weather outlasts much cooler times, we tend to ride around most of the year with the windows up.

Lately, however, I've been letting the windows of my car down while I am driving and letting the fresh air in—and everything else. I am surprised that it has taken me so long to not care about bugs flying in, my hair flying about, and the sound of other people's music blaring as loudly as it does on television shows when some director is trying to prove that a certain kind of other driver is oblivious to taking up too much space in public by riding around with the music blaring.

I don't mind the young with their rocking music encroaching on my space—coming through my open car windows with a beat that is a form of music I don't like very much. Play it anyway. Let me hear what you like even if I don't understand why. I need fresh music the way I am presently craving fresh air.

It is a new sensation, this. With the same intensity that I have starved for solitude most of my life, I am hungry for whatever might blow in on the wind.

So in addition to riding around now in still warm temperatures with the air conditioning on and my car windows down, I also live with my windows open at home. Sure, it's the allergy season—it's always the allergy season. But I find that for a couple of hours in the morning, airing out my house is worth the potential itchiness that could follow. I want to have the fresh smell of the outdoors inside for the rest of the day and the evacuation of yesterday's once good aromas that now only smell stale: old bacon, old toast, old popcorn.

I'd rather smell tea olive and gardenia and hear the neighbors shout or pull their trash cans in and know when the mail has arrived and where the mail carrier is on her route as she moves from the street behind me to mine and then on to the next street where my oldest niece Lola lives with her husband and two-year old son, spending her days in the domestic routine that suits her better than the professional life she gave up did, I think.

When the windows of my house are open I am closer to Lola…close enough to hear her come up the drive way when she and her son take a walk around the block and detour to Aunt Daphne's house. With the widows open, I can hear her when she calls out "Hello. Anybody home?"

How lovely to stop whatever I am doing—it is never very important—and throw back that door and find them there, two different expressions on their faces: his, intense: `where are my Crayons, my stacking cups, the piano?' ;hers, 'are we bothering you?'

I press my face against Lola's (named after her grandmother of sweet potato pie fame) cheek and smell the fresh air on her skin, marveling that she gets more beautiful by the day as her boy gets taller. Jon takes off through the house, oblivious to whether the floor needs to be mopped or just has been, and we follow him along on his route as he touches bases: yes, the Crayons are still there but there's a new coloring book, and there are his stacking cups, and the piano can still make the sounds of "Twinkle, Twinkle." His mother and I sit down and let him make his small journey that reminds him that all is as it was and should be, while she and I make the kind of small talk that is more important than earth-shattering news or religious revelations.

I'm grading papers.

She's preparing for a baby shower for her sister-in-law, Renee.

I have just baked a Butter Pecan cake.

She'd love a piece.

I haven't heard from my publisher yet.

Time passes slowly when you're waiting, but too fast when you are raising a child you adore.

We eat cake and drink some lemonade, adding fresh cubes to Jon's sippy cup that he can, with delight, shake like maracas.

"Have you had your windows open?" Lola asks, looking around approvingly. She does not notice that I have not dusted. She sees her grandmother's oak table and her thoughts shift in and out of time but not sadly. As if paging through a family album or walking past the series of family photos on the way, her mind can move through time backwards while living in the present. She knows now that while the world measures time mostly in that linear way—chronologically—that human time and human experience is so much bigger and not confined at all to any one moment in time you can point to and say, "There is life. I am looking at it right now." It feels like that when you are growing up, but when you are older you no longer think as a child only—and you don't give up being a child. You learn how to integrate the child of your past into the age of your present and on into the future.

Lola is old enough to move in and out of time in the tempo of homage to the past while looking ahead with gusto– to live with her windows open, too. We tell each other the truth in simple ways.

"Yes," I say, contentment filling me in ways that are deeper than that one word can express. "I have had the windows open all day. The air is fresh, the leaves are turning. The light outside looks different."

"The season is changing," she agrees, smiling, and when she does I see her simultaneously in a season now and apart from it too–as a child forever, as ageless as a bride who stays in love her whole marriage, as a mother who is beginning to know that she will always have all of the ages of her son inside of her now and for as long as she lives.

She asks me, her eyes bright with love and the light of changing seasons, "What's for supper?"

Section 10
YOUR SIGNATURE DISH

What's in this section:

Mildred Budge's Signature Jelly Cake

Pineapple Filling

Mildred Budge's Favorite Almond-Flavored Pound Cake

Mildred Budge's Butter Pecan Cake

Aunt Daphne's Christmas Fudge

Aunt Daphne's Fudge Topping for Ice Cream

Your Mama's Signature Pecan Pie

Aunt Daphne's Chocolate Chip Pie

Aunt Julie's Coffee Cake

Cousin Kevin's Simple White Sauce

Guin's Date Loaf Candy

Cousin Lola's Chocolate Chip Muffins

At Home Everywhere I Go: *The Bride's Room*

Beloved,

I am thinking about your signature colors.

Like the colors of pink and yellow that you chose for your wedding scheme, your signature dish will be chosen too over time, and when people think of you they might think of that dish the way they remember the colors you like. There are all sorts of details that remind other people of who we are, and we like having these sorts of preferences signal to others: I like pink. I like yellow. I like fudge.

So, it made sense to me that when I began to write a series of books about a fictional character, Mildred Budge—a church lady of the South who is a retired fifth grade school teacher–that she would be able to cook the way the women in our family cook and that she would have many signature dishes, like we all have, really.

I made up Mildred Budge, and I made up the recipe for jelly cake, which is the first dish associated with her in the first novel, **Cloverdale**. Her last name is significant. Her last name is Budge. I use her whole name sometimes as a play on midriff bulge, but the exploration of the word "budge" also refers to our need to change and keep changing—improving–that wars against our desire to stay put and to be satisfied with the status quo. We call that a routine. Routines are sometimes useful but not always. It is difficult to strike a balance and find the wisdom of staying put when we need to stay a course and changing our minds and our attitudes when we need to do that. It doesn't have to be very important to get our attention. Sometimes we are first aware of a desire to change when we begin to say too often, "I'm bored" or "I'm tired." Listen closely and observe very carefully that many people use that expression as a cry for help rather than a description of a need for rest or sleep.

People don't always say what they mean. Mildred Budge most often says what she means. I like that about her. But she also keeps her own counsel—doesn't offer too many opinions unnecessarily. Our opinions are not as necessary to others as we like to believe, and our opinions are not the same as facts, though many people cannot tell the difference between their opinion and a fact.

Mildred Budge can. Mildred Budge is a good cook, but she's not a great cook. She will try to cook anything, and in a current novel I am writing, **The Bride's Room,** she is trying to perfect the perfect recipe for a wedding cake—an activity I enjoyed once upon a time in real life not so long ago. It is a lovely quest to pursue a wonderful invention of a recipe that fits an occasion and appetites.

I call this a quest. I went on one to replicate your grandmother's missing recipe for sweet potato pie, and I have been on other quests, too. While writing this collection of recipes for you I am also working on discovering the perfect recipe for a creamy vanilla fudge. I like vanilla fudge. I do not know why I have waited so long to try and make it. Maybe it is because my chocolate fudge is so good. That sounds just like your grandmother.

In the third Mildred Budge novel she will be baking a wedding cake for a good friend. Mildred finds out, as I discovered when I baked a wedding cake for your mother, that the portions of wedding cakes as envisioned for guests is quite small—truly, a small sliver of a cake, which I think is completely wrong! If there is ever a time to have lots and lots of cake and to eat lots and lots of cake it is a wedding party. But Mildred Budge and I appear to be alone in that philosophy.

When baking a cake you will frequently run into the term "let the ingredients reach room temperature." This term often applies to eggs when you are baking a pound cake of some kind or butter which you need to be able to blend easily but don't want melted. That phrase "room temperature" is an important one, and I hope that when you see it in the future you will think about this. It is Mildred Budge's view of what room temperature really means.

Aunt Mildred's View of Room Temperature

"When a recipe calls for an ingredient to be brought out and left to become set at room temperature, remember that human beings have a love affair with the status quo. That's a kind of room temperature of your life, and it takes a while to figure out that most of the circumstances around us wax hot and cold. It is a rare season in your life that fits the human inclination for status quo—room temperature. If you do reach that routine, which happens from time to time, you will find yourself growing restless, desiring a change. Sometimes that desire will take you to someone else's yard where the grass is reportedly greener, but no one else's life or yard is better than your own life built upon thoughtful choices. Do not assume that when you feel restless or bored something is wrong that needs to be fixed. There are times in your life when you simply feel like you're at room temperature and sometimes that feels secure and wonderful or boring and unbearable for much longer.

When those feelings happen, go bake something that calls for the eggs or the butter to reach room temperature before you can use them. Then, smile. There is no need to do something drastic right away. Test your feelings of discontent, boredom or even a love affair with routine, and then prayerfully work your way through it.

That is the way of a lifetime—not just a way to handle something one time.

Life is filled with shifting emotions and rising and falling temperatures. Don't react to that any more strongly than you would the weather outside that also changes."

Mildred Budge's Signature Jelly Cake (This could be any cake that would be complemented by jelly. Mildred Budge favors homemade preserves made by a woman named Mrs. Parsons, who not only cans her own preserves and jams but often grows the fruit that she uses to make her jellies.)

The cake's ingredients:

2 cups sugar

½ cup butter

3 eggs

2 cups flour

2 teaspoons baking powder

⅛ teaspoon salt

1 cup milk

1 teaspoon vanilla extract

Directions:

Cream sugar and butter. Add eggs. Then, add dry ingredients alternately with milk. Add Vanilla extract. Put batter in two 9-inch greased layer cake pans. Bake at 350 degrees about 30-35 minutes or until the cake springs back when lightly touched.

If you don't have a good jar of jelly or preserves, you can make this filling.

Pineapple Filling

Ingredients:

1 large can crushed pineapple

1 cup sugar

1 tablespoon flour

⅛ teaspoon salt

4 teaspoons butter.

Directions:

Mix all ingredients and cook until thick. Spread on cooled cake. Enough for two layers.

Mildred Budge's Favorite Almond-Flavored Pound Cake

Ingredients:

2 sticks of butter

3 cups of sugar

3 cups of all-purpose flour

½ teaspoon baking powder

¼ teaspoon salt

6 eggs

1 cup of whole milk

½ teaspoon vanilla extract

½ teaspoon almond extract

Directions: Mix the flour, baking powder and salt together and set aside.

In a large mixing bowl, cream the butter and the sugar. Add the eggs one at a time, beating well after each addition. Then, add your flour mixture in small amounts, alternating with milk until you get it all combined. Then, add your extracts.

Pour the batter into a greased and floured Bundt pan. Bake at 350 degrees for about an hour and fifteen minutes. It will be crusty, and people like that about it.

Mildred Budge's Butter Pecan Cake

Ingredients you will need:

3 tablespoons of melted butter in which you will toast the pecans

1 and a half cups of pecans –coarsely chopped (a cup for the cake and a half cup for the frosting) I actually usually toast about two cups of these pecans because I nibble on them while I cook. It reduces the anxiety of whether you will have enough if you just make more than the recipe calls for.

A good cup of butter softened for the cake recipe—This recipe runs dry to me so I usually toss in any extra chunks of butter sitting on saucers in the refrigerator. I feel no guilt about this, and I have never had it too buttery.

1 generous cup of white sugar

2-3 eggs (I use three eggs.)

2 generous cups all-purpose flour

1 ½ teaspoon baking powder

¼ teaspoon salt

⅔ cup of fresh whole milk for the cake- don't tamper with the taste of this cake by going low-fat milk—

1 ½ teaspoon vanilla extract

Frosting

½ cup of softened butter

3 cups or more of Confectioner's sugar—I keep the bag of sugar handy in case it doesn't look like enough frosting, and I like a lot of frosting between the layers.

3-4 tablespoons of fresh whole milk

A scant teaspoon of Vanilla extract

A half cup of pecans, toasted

To begin: Melt three tablespoons of butter in a large 9 x 13 Pyrex dish. Stir in the pecans until they are coated in butter. Bake them at 350 degrees, stirring if you are nervous about scorching them. I stir them about five minutes into it. Let them cool while you prepare the batter. Try to resist them. It's hard.

For the cake: Cream the softened butter in a large mixing bowl and add the sugar. Add the eggs slowly just like your mother taught you, one at a time. Don't rush it. Beat well after every addition just the way you do a pound cake.

Mix the flour, baking powder, and salt in another bowl and then begin to add this mixture to your creamed sugar, adding the milk to keep it moist and reduce the flour dust that blows.

Stir in the Vanilla extract and a cup of the toasted pecans. Remember to reserve about a half cup of the pecans for the frosting.

Pour your batter evenly into two greased and floured 9-inch layer pans. Bake at 350 degrees for about 30 minutes. Press on the middle with your forefinger. If it bounces back, you're fine. Or do the toothpick test.

Cool the cake. Remove from pans. Cool while you make your frosting.

The frosting:

This frosting is a variation on that theme of butter cream frosting you most likely grew up making.

Directions:

Begin with your butter—about a half cup to start. If you like a lot of frosting, increase the amount of butter and then add more sugar. I beat the butter, add the vanilla, and then add the Confectioner's sugar with small additions of milk, and watch it grow. The thickness of the frosting depends upon how much milk you add. I don't like it too thick or too thin, like a glaze. And, I almost always make twice as much frosting as a recipe calls for and still don't feel like there's enough between the layers. When you have as much frosting as you think you will need, stir in the remaining toasted pecans. You might even want to keep some to dust on the top. I do.

It's a pretty cake that impresses other people. However, this cake doesn't keep longer than two days without beginning to taste dry. Fortunately, people like it so much it doesn't usually last longer than two days.

Tip: Without the pecans, Mildred and I agree that this would make a very pretty wedding cake.

Aunt Daphne's Christmas Fudge (recipe from Hershey's)

I am most famous for my fudge. Success rests upon how you heat the mixture up, how long you stir the fudge, and how much you like to eat fudge, for many times people fail at making a recipe because they do not really enjoy food or like the dish they are making.

I really like fudge though not as much as I once did.

Here's the recipe.

Ingredients:

A lump of butter to generously grease the fudge platter with

½ stick of butter to add at the end

¾ cup cocoa

3 cups sugar

1 ½ cups whole milk

Dash of salt

Pecans—a cup or so, chopped

Thick-glass platter

1 teaspoon vanilla extract

Directions:

Start with a heavy-bottomed tallish saucepan because fudge boils up and then goes down, and it needs that room to rise without spilling over onto the range.

Begin with putting your dry ingredients in the pan. Stir them well before you ever turn on the heat. Then, add the milk and begin to heat the mixture slowly. Doing it slowly means that the sugar dissolves well.

Slowly bring to a medium high boil. It will go up and then go back down—takes a few minutes. When the fudge does go down, the bubbles will be denser and smaller. Reduce the heat a notch or two and begin to watch it. Keep a cup of cold water at the ready and frequently test the mixture to see if it is making a soft ball by dropping a small amount in the bottom of the cold water. If it goes splat, it's not ready. When the drop of fudge keeps the shape of a drop, press it with you finger lightly and see if it retains that shape. I do this about three times before I trust it, and then I remove the fudge from the stove. Add the butter—a half stick—and a teaspoon of vanilla extract. Stir. Stir. Beat. Let cool a bit. Stir and beat some more. When it begins to thicken, add the nuts. Pour the mixture onto the platter. Let cool a bit. When it is firm but not completely set, slice it. If you wait until it is too firm, you can't slice it without breaking it and the slices are not as pretty.

You can make a version of this taste as a fudge topping for ice cream. Here's that version:

Fudge topping for ice cream and for using as a dip for fresh fruit

What you need:

About three heaping tablespoons of cocoa (I don't actually measure it.)

About a cup of sugar.

A dash of salt

A small can of evaporated milk or 1/3 cup whole milk

Some white Karo syrup—I pour some from the bottle, probably a half cup or so. I don't measure this either.

A lump of good butter—about three tablespoons, I guess. I don't measure this.

A half teaspoon of vanilla extract.

Directions:

In a small saucepan, add about three tablespoons of cocoa and about a quarter cup or so (maybe a half) white Karo syrup. Add a small can of evaporated milk. Add a dash of salt. Stir and slowly bring to a boil. Let it boil a minute. Remove from heat. Add about a half teaspoon of Vanilla extract. Let cool while you eat your supper. Then, when you serve ice cream for dessert, place this pan on the table and let people help themselves to it with big spoons to add to their ice cream.

Your Mama's Signature Pecan Pie

Start with a prepared pie crust that you have forked sufficiently so that it will cook through.

For the filling for pecan pie, you need:

1 cup Karo Syrup

3 eggs

1 cup sugar

2 tablespoons butter, melted

1 teaspoon vanilla extract

1 ½ cups pecans

Directions:

Blend the first five ingredients and add the pecans. I think your mama cooks this gently first. Pour into pie and bake. Do this on a cookie sheet in case it runs over.

Aunt Daphne's Chocolate Chip Pie

Ingredients:

1 cup sugar

½ cup all-purpose flour

2 lightly beaten eggs

1 stick butter, melted and cooled

1 cup of chopped pecans

1 6 ounce package of semi-sweet chocolate chips

1 teaspoon vanilla extract

A prepared pie crust.

Directions:

Mix your sugar and flour. Add the other ingredients. Pour it all into a pie crust and bake for about an hour.

Aunt Julie's Signature Coffee Cake

Ingredients:

¼ cup plain flour

⅓ cup brown sugar

2 tablespoons butter or margarine

1 teaspoon cinnamon

½ cup nuts (optional)

1 yellow cake mix

Directions:

Prepare the cake mix according to the directions on the box. Pour into two prepared layer pans. Blend all other ingredients and sprinkle on the batter. Bake as directed on the mix's box.

Cousin Kevin's Simple White Sauce

On one of those nights at the end of the month, make fettuccine or any other noodle with white sauce.

You need:

Milk

½ cup of Parmesan cheese

Salt and pepper

Bring a cup of milk slowly to a simmer and add a half cup of grated Parmesan cheese. Let it melt. Pour over any cooked noodles.

Guin's Date Loaf Candy, which she makes at Christmas

Ingredients:

2 cups of sugar

1 small can of evaporated milk

1 package of pitted, chopped dates

A generous cup of coarsely chopped pecans

½ stick of butter (maybe a little less)

Directions:

In a tallish saucepan bring the sugar and milk slowly to a gentle boil. Add the dates and cook to a soft ball stage. I have never had a thermometer that worked well for this thick mixture, so I drop bits of the cooking candy in cold water in a shallow coffee cup and watch until it congeals to a soft ball. Reach through the cold water and touch the candy. If it holds together, it's fine. Then cook just a few more seconds and remove from heat. Add the nuts and the butter and stir. Sometimes the butter is more than I need and I scoop out the last bit.

Are you asking yourself if I have forgotten the Vanilla extract? I haven't. It doesn't need it. I tried adding it once and the taste did not improve. This recipe comes from Miss Esther who lived on a farm, and the key to this recipe for her was that she always had the ingredients on hand. That's the test of a really good recipe.

Pour the cooling mixture onto a damp T-towel laid out on a cookie sheet that will brace it. Then, roll the sides of the towel up and shape into a pleasing loaf. Mine is usually about four to five inches wide and about eight inches long. I take it out on the back porch and let it cool.

Then, after supper I bring it in and slice it a piece at a time to serve. When it has set, I transfer the loaf of candy from the now very sticky T-towel to waxed paper and then wrap the candy in tin foil. Refrigerate if you prefer, but the candy slices better at room temperature. It's too much candy for one person to eat so find yourself a friend and share it.

Cousin Lola's Chocolate Chip Muffins

Makes one dozen regular muffins

Ingredients

1 ½ cups unbleached, all-purpose flour

2 t baking powder

½ t salt

¼ c canola or vegetable oil

⅓ c (scant) granulated sugar

⅓ c lightly packed dark brown sugar

1 egg

1 ½ t vanilla

1 ¼ c semi-sweet chocolate morsels (a bit more if you like)

Directions:

Grease with butter or lightly coat with non-stick spray one standard-size muffin tin. Set aside.

In a large bowl, whisk together flour, baking powder, and salt. Combine well and set aside.

Preheat oven to 400 degrees.

Using a whisk, beat oil and both sugars in medium bowl until well combined. Add egg and vanilla and mix well.

Add wet ingredients to dry ingredients and stir only until all dry ingredients are moistened. Do not over mix! Stir in chocolate morsels.

Filling each muffin cup about half full should yield a perfect dozen muffins. Bake at 400 degrees for 17-20 minutes. Muffins are done when edges appear golden brown and tops spring back lightly.

Lola says:

"This recipe really does create muffins—i.e., not chocolate chip cupcakes. The texture, if prepared correctly, should fall somewhere between a cupcake and a scone.

I have experimented with both the type of chocolate morsels I use and the type of fat. I have found that different types of fat (e.g., unsalted butter or coconut oil) create desirable alternatives in the flavor profile but can affect the texture, moisture, and bake time for the muffins, so try the recipe with oil the first time. Differing types and brands of chocolate chips, of course, also affect the flavor profile and can be chosen based on the cook's preference for level of sweetness, cocoa content, and so forth without affecting the texture of the muffin."

At Home Everywhere I Go....

The Bride's Room

Once or twice a year I spend the hour of regular worship service in what is typically called the prayer parlor. On weddings days, however, when a bride occupies that room waiting to be escorted down the aisle, it is called the Bride's Room. When I take my turn praying, I think of all the brides who have spent a few hours there dressed in an outfit that proclaimed to the world "I am the bride."

I imagine too that my Presbyterian preacher thinks that I am sitting ladylike in the prayer chair earnestly praying for the service. I get around to sitting still when it is my turn to pray for the worship service; but at first, I get my bearings. I walk around the room. Standing in front of a series of carefully crafted drawings, I experience Melissa Tubbs' exquisite work on the wall. They are architectural drawings of specific locations of this building. Deceptively austere, they draw you into not the place they represent but into a timelessness, a serenity so peaceful that I can hear the whisper from heaven, "Be still and know that I am God." In those pictures I enter that stillness and know a deeper way of breathing, of being, but once I turn away I find myself wondering about the artist who captured those still moments. I deduce that the artist has a pure heart, and I wonder what that feels like and if she sees God. The Bible says that pure-hearted people do.

Looking around me, I see that the parlor floor is clean, the room more than tidy—it is orderly. The schedule of how to pray is on the far right table, and I will pick it up soon; but before I do, I wonder if someone has added more envisioned necessary items to the side drawer in a small end table over by the sofa. The first time I took my turn in the prayer parlor years ago I looked inside that drawer, expecting to find a Kleenex and did, but I also found a sewing kit, a Band-Aid, a lip liner (mauve), some clear nail polish to repair hosiery, a small hair brush, a comb, a traveler's size bottle of hairspray, some Scotch tape, and a bottle of Tylenol. Some woman– or women–supplied that drawer with the kinds of accessory tools that a bride might need when she is dressing and waiting in this room with her mother, her grandmother, her best friends and maybe her favorite aunt. Fearing she might see her groom before the appointed time, she wouldn't leave the Bride's Room. It was all there—anything that a seasoned bride could imagine a new bride might need on her wedding day.

I have never been in this prayer parlor when it became the Bride's Room, but I have enjoyed this room as a bride myself. I feel like one when it is my turn to pray for the church.

It is my favorite activity at church—the sweetest time I know in that building. Eventually, I pick up the laundry list of prayer requests designed by someone whose theology is well-schooled and intact. I cannot sit still easily when I pray that list. I must move around the room, reading the Bible, consulting the list, and occasionally asking Jesus, "What's your pleasure?" It is one of my favorite prayers. Fancier people might call this activity intercessory prayer. I don't know what my preacher would call it. I experience the prayer time as an inviolate space of communion and quiet where I, by the Bridegroom's invitation and not just because the preacher asks it of the members here, whisper sweet somethings back to the Eternal Lover of mankind. He is the very reason we have a worship service. He is always listening.

It is such a happy, peaceful room, filled with hope, prayers and the kinds of memories that someone who shows up to pray hears in a similar way to the awareness that I keep of the worship service I faintly hear on the other side of the wall. Finally, up from lying prostrate on the clean rug, my arms outstretched—and I don't remember deciding to take that posture– I eventually sit upright in the prayer chair and take deep draughts of those echoes of bridal parties that live in the room while I am there whispering to Jesus about the worship service happening in the sanctuary, and smiling, smiling, asking, asking in a kind of murmur that sounds in my ears like a gurgling brook, "What's your pleasure, my Heart's Desire?"

The Eternal Bridegroom whispers to me in a voice that old and young brides learn to hear, and which, upon hearing, makes the light of the prayer parlor suffuse that space—both the room and me. In the suffusion of that light and in the sweet and undeniable whisper of that One who has gone to build another place for us—if it were not so, he would have told us!—I wait for him as all do who hear that voice and have said, "I do."

In that instant of saying "I do" I came alive and move about now and have my being forever and always in the eternal Bride's Room. Those who live outside the Bride's Room cannot imagine what the room is like. Not really.

Even those of us who have spent a good deal of time in the Light-Suffused Space are still learning its features the way an artist studies her subject—carefully assessing the layout of the room– and trying to build a vocabulary to help understand and name the functions of the furnishings. As we acquire more tools in the Bride's Room, we are also trying to let go of what we don't need—trying to learn how to give up trying to measure aspects of this life that exist apart from that kind of assessment, like time. Unlike the array of tools in that small drawer by the sofa in the prayer parlor that are so easy to name and explain, the furnishings of the eternal Bride's Room exist as inherited promises, live inside God-ordained assurances, and ultimately, though we have entered a new kind of stillness called his rest, we can't stay motionless for long. We keep turning, turning, turning to the sound of that Bridegroom's voice that never really stops whispering proposals that have different endings but all seem to begin with "Come unto me...."

It is a good and mysterious and romantic life living inside the eternal Bride's Room that many call by other names just as we call the prayer parlor the Bride's Room when a bride is using it for the day. The space we live inside the faith of having said 'yes' to Love is sometimes called kingdom life, being saved, and perhaps the most intriguing, green pastures: endless green pastures as expansive as eternity but where the threshold is always narrow and monogamously defined by one Bridegroom: Jesus. You cannot cross over into the green pastures without saying yes to his proposal of unconditional love. Some people don't hear him that way, but I hear that invitation.

In a post-Enlightenment time when technology has put humanity on notice of sorts that parts of who we are as humans may well be obsolete (not true), the sustaining beauty of green pastures ruled by an Invisible Shepherd seems incongruous to those who do not stop to listen for his voice. People like me who live there report that we have heard him, and like some last frontier that has not yet been fully explored, we report the great pleasures and adventure of it, but we are often not believed. Although the testimonies of so many voices that claim to have experienced so many other kinds of invisible truths are readily acceptable in many instances, there is an odd resistance to those believers who have heard the Bridegroom's invitation, said yes, and walked across the threshold into a honeymoon of sorts and called over their shoulders: "It's lovely here. Come and see for yourself."

That invitation is very much like tossing a bridal bouquet to waiting people who want love, too—say so with hands reaching out, grasping for any kind of love in spite of epidemic divorce rates and untold heartbreak.

I have been a Christian for most of my life, and it is still fresh and intimate and satisfying and increasingly, as I approach an age of potential infirmity and my own certain death, I am more and more hopeful. I am a technologically adept, Enlightenment-versed, respecter of science and logic, and I illogically wake up happy every day in these green pastures and hear an invisible Shepherd say in so many ways: "Come unto me...."

Every day I accept.

And every day, in its Christ-held way, is a good day.

I have been loved well by the Eternal Bridegroom—he has kept his promises, and I have not always kept mine. When that has happened, I have said so to him (those moments are called repentance), and he has heard me and said again and again, "Come back. I'm still right here."

He always is– waiting on the threshold where he has always been–beckoning, inviting, waiting, arms outstretched iconically not only as a bridegroom waiting for the bride at the end of an aisle but like a father in a field waiting on a prodigal child to remember Love Is and turn, turn, return. It is a big place—those green pastures that are also a Bride's Room—a space that is intimate and romantic and big enough for everyone.

Come and see.

Beloved,

You went off to college, made "A's", and confessed that you wanted to be a hair stylist, and so you went to Beauty School. I followed you to Beauty School because I saw your other stylists-to-be friends practicing their techniques on mannequin heads. Although I did remember how your granddaddy wanted to buy you mannequins for company once upon a time, I did not want you to practice only on a lifeless head, so I sat in your chair while you learned the art of coloring and cutting and we talked of beauty—and there is so much to say. We did not get to Aristotle or Keats, and I did not get to tell you about a room where your mother and my sisters grew up called The Beauty Room, which your grandfather built for us—a place appointed for five women to do their hair together and we did once upon a time. But during your days in the Beauty School we began a conversation about beauty, which I suspect we will continue for the rest of our lives.

I knew though from sitting in that chair as you practiced on me while learning your craft—and stopped spontaneously, joyfully, to dance with your friends when the music they were playing changed–that you would touch lives by making people who came to you feel good about themselves. Human touch is powerful. Ideas are, too. And prayer works.

You graduated at the top of your class from Beauty School and began your full-time job at that posh salon in Atlanta. Then, I blinked, and you had fallen in love, and and eloped to Las Vegas and said "I do" becoming a part of "You.....Me" that is the theme of love, marriage and living happily ever after. Most people think that this last description is part of a fairy tale that no longer exists as real or practical for thinking people living in a world struggling with terrorism, a bad economy and other dynamics that do not create the kind of idealistic framework that people believe is necessary for a marriage to succeed, but I think they are wrong. Integrate the concept of trouble into daily life and face it with the truths from the Bible, and you will live happily ever after and after and after.....

You changed your last name, Katie, but your name is on my speed dial the same way it always has been. No matter where you go, what you study, and what you cook and how many other people are joining you at your dining table in any part of the world where you are living as a military wife, when you are answering the question, "What's for supper?" your name stays the same to me because the way I feel about you will never change except to grow stronger and stronger over time– Katie Beloved.

Aunt Daphne

About the gatherer of the recipes

About Aunt Daphne: I like to cook and I like to write. To learn more about me, visit my website: www.daphnesimpkins.com The Mildred Budge books are available through any bookstore and in online bookstores. The titles are: **Miss Budge in Love** (a collection of short stories)**, Cloverdale** and **Embankment**. Unless I change my mind, the next novel featuring Miss Budge will be called **The Bride's Room.**

Made in the USA
Columbia, SC
04 April 2019